DONALD E CARTER

THE SHIELD OF ZEUS

THE SHIELD OF ZEUS

THE SHIELD OF ZEUS

Copyright © 2025 by donald E carter
All rights reserved. No part of this book may be reproduced in any manner whatsoever without written permission except in the case of brief quotations embodied in critical articles and reviews.
First Printing, 2025

CONTENTS

The shield of Zeus
v

1 — Camp
1

2 — The Parthenon
8

3 — Temple of the Olympian Zeus
26

4 — The Temple of Zeus
50

5 — Statue of Zeus
69

6 — Mt.Rainier
98

7 — An end to ends
124

8 — a goodnight's rest
132

THE SHIELD OF ZEUS

Conclusion info
135
sneak peek
136
About the Author
137

CAMP

"Zack, are you alright?" one of my friends in a seat next to me asked. I looked at her and nodded and said "I will be fine."

At that very moment we had arrived at our destination and our teacher Mr. Deoak stood up followed by Mr. Demp and ordered everyone off the bus.

When we were all off the bus Mr.Demp stayed behind as the others left to go into the museum.

We started off the bus and as we were getting off mr. demp eyed us like we were doing something wrong and then we had gone inside to take a look inside the museum.

When we got inside the first thing I noticed was the statues of Zeus, Hades, and Poseidon with a plaque that was labled "the big three". Before I knew it, I was being nudged along because without knowing it I was staring at the one that said "Zeus,the king of the gods".

Even after I had started moving along, I still couldn't get his face out of my head.

It was like we had this connection kind of like I knew him but that was impossible right? The Greek gods weren't real.

I just had to figure this out, so I ran to catch up to the others with my friend on my heels until we had caught up to our substitute teacher Mr.Deoak and the class.

I put on my earphones and started to listen to music until the class started to walk to the next exhibit and then all of a sudden a mist came into the museum but it seemed like nobody else noticed.

Then I saw movement out of the corner of my eye and I saw Mr.Demp moving towards me and he bent forward into my ear and told me to follow him.

I started to follow him and as soon as I got into the next room I saw a flash of smoke out of the corner of my eye and turned to look at it but there was nothing there and my teacher was gone as well.

I looked all around then then I saw him in the corner of the room and he came up to me but he didn't look the same way that he did when we got off the bus, now he had long red spikes coming out of his shoulders and now that I got a good look at him he also had a long curved scorpion tail and an extra four legs coming out of his torso

He had turned into a monster of some sort and then he started yelling at me saying" where is it? Where is the shield of Zeus; I know that you have it."

Then he started to attack me with his scorpion tail and

even picked me up and threw me back against the wall. I went to run away but he swung his tail right in my way blocking the doorway.

Then he turned his gaze at the door because at that moment Mr. Deoak came into the room and started saying" get back". The monster said "you" and went out an archway to the left.

The door opened again and in came my friend that was next to me on the bus and said, "it's finally happened hasn't it?"

Mr. Deoak said to my friend "he must go now, go home and tell his mom and I'll meet you there." At that moment he turned to me and started pulling me towards the entrance and kept muttering under his breath "I must take him to camp... I must take him to camp.

Then he turned to me and said " it's a matter of life or death" and he gave me what at first glance looked like a gold marker then he turned and we started to run home and found my mom in the kitchen baking and then my friend told my mom "Zack has to go...and I mean he has to go now."

We got into her car which was a sixty-four Cadillac coupe de Ville and started to drive away from the city for an hour until we were driving down a road laden with trees on the side as far as the eye could see.

I asked my mom where we were and my mom said" we are on the way to the camp that your dad started. It's the only place where you'll be safe ."

I turned to her and asked her "my dad, what do you mean?" Then all of a sudden my mom started to swerve from side to side and then she swerved and came to a stop and then all of a sudden the car went flying and when we came to a stop I looked around and saw something moving and then I got a good look at it and saw that it was a cyclopes and it was running right for us.

I looked around for my friend but soon found out that my friend was already out of the car and was reaching for my hand and I gratefully took it and looked around for my mom to see her going to the woods my mom started to run for the woods and she motioned for us to hurry after her.

As we got farther into the forest, I could hear it after us and then I saw an archway that said camp demi-god and I went through the archway like there was nothing there.

However as my mom tried to go through it the arch would block her way so I pulled and pulled but it was no use, I tried to pull her through once more and then my mom said Zack go.. I can't follow you, you are meant to go forward.

By that time the cyclops had caught up and picked my mom up and she exploded in a ball of light and disappeared.

In a blind rage I went up to the cyclopes and my friend said" pull the lid off the marker". As I did it became a bronze short sword and after that things started to get a little hazy.

THE SHIELD OF ZEUS

I remember blocking a throw by the monster and then it pushed me and I lost ahold of the sword and it started to go after me again then I saw the sword and it was a few inches from my feet so as the cyclopes came running at me again I raised my sword and the monster screamed in agony and then in a flash of bright light it was gone but so was my mom and then I passed out.

A couple hours must have passed because when I awoke it was morning and I was laying on some type of bed and there was yelling outside so I went outside into the bright sunlight and what I saw was a bunch of kids sword fighting and then I saw the other teacher that was on the bus with us so I went up to him and said "so you're a centaur Mr. Deoak" and he said back to me" in our land I'm called Chiron".

Then he turned his gaze to the others and said" as you might have heard the Greek gods' artifacts have been lost and it is time that they be assembled and put back in their rightful owners hands or the titans will rise again."

Then he pulled out a hat and asked everyone to put a paper with their name on it and put it in the hat. Once everyone had done so he reached into the hat and said "the demi-god that will be going to go to find the artifacts will be Zack Ryan".

Then he reached into another hat that I'm guessing already had names in it and said" the satyr that goes with Zack is Danyelle Quinn" and a lady satyr stood up and I noticed that it was the girl that was my friend from the bus.

She walked over to me and said" so I guess we are on this quest together... we had better talk to Chiron about the details". We walked up to the hill where he was and knocked on the wooden door and went up to Chiron.

As we went up to him he turned around and looked at us and said "I presume that you need to know where to start?" we nodded then gave us a map that already had the first location on it and it read: the Parthenon.

Then he handed over a bag and said" these are very powerful marbles all you have to do is roll it and visualize where it is that you want to go and it instantly opens a portal to that place but first you have to pay a drachma to understand it?"

We nodded and then he said "Oh...and two more things, you need a warrior by your side, someone who you can count on and is wise. So that means it has to be a child of Athena, so you have two options and he pointed towards a boy about seventeen and said: Athero.

Then he pointed to a girl looked rather fierce about the same age said"or Athenesta." So I pointed at the guy because he looked like he could carry his own weight.

As he walked over he gave a smile at the young woman and walked over and Chiron said: "good choice with Athero but you could have done better with Athenesta"and there will be seven pieces to Zeus's shield, so good luck.

Then he rolled the first marble, and we visualized the Parthenon in Greece how we thought it would be because we had never been there, and then he Athero threw a gold drachma into the portal and we went through right into the bright sunshine.

As we arrived, the sun was going down, and we set up camp. The next morning we went into the Parthenon and soon we noticed that there was what seemed to be a crack in the far wall with something behind it so we moved what seemed to be an old tarp off the wall to find a mark on the wall partly showing behind the crack so I picked up a big branch and pried the rest of it off to reveal the symbol of the shield of Zeus.

As we peeled the rest of it off, we saw it glowed and Athero touched it and got pulled into it, so we had no choice. We had to go in after him.

CHAPTER 2

THE PARTHENON

When we landed, we hit hard, and we slid down a slanted hallway and we all landed in a heap on top of the other.

When we got up, Athero and I started looking around and the first thing that we noticed was the writing on the walls that appeared as we were watching

We watched it until it finished. Then I noticed Danyelle was coming up right next to me and we all read together: down this hall and hang a right to follow that hall then step into the light, go across the clearing and find a waterfall and behind it there will be your first clue.

We went around the room looking for a hallway but couldn't find one and then Athero stepped on a stone and it went down.

As his foot went down, a doorway opened up. We all looked at each other in astonishment at him and all he did was grin stupidly. We walked up to the door, but the door closed as soon as his foot left, so we hurried on through to the other side.

Once the door was closed behind us, we laughed out loud and soon noticed that we were in a long hallway and so we followed it. Soon we had to go in single file into a bigger hallway that almost immediately turned right and came into a clearing that was huge. So huge, in fact, that it looked like a mansion could fit inside of it.

When we stepped into it we noticed it had like a light of some sort and we went to searching for the last part of the clue but after an hour of searching we almost gave up and then Danyelle started staring at the wall and so I said "what are you looking at"? but she ignored me and walked up to the wall and started pulling off vines and before long she had a weird mechanism uncovered.

We walked up and looked it over and then out of the blue, Athero said, "I think it's a puzzle, but what does it go to, I wonder?"

We looked around for something that was of any relation to the puzzle then I saw a piece of metal sticking out of the ground with the same shape as the puzzle but we still didn't have anywhere to put it in so I pulled it up and hung onto it.

Although I discovered a third lever component (without realizing it), two more remained to be found. A yell quickly followed. Danyelle ran up to me, yelling and waving a lever piece, exclaiming, "See what I found!"

An hour passed, and we were still looking for the bottom of the lever and then suddenly I saw a glimmer out of the corner of my eye so I went up to it and saw that it was a diamond with a shape like the end of one piece so I tested it out.

I put together the two pieces that I had and, like magnets, they sucked together. Then I called Danyelle over and had her put her piece with it and we now had our handle, but we still didn't know where to put it.

We started looking on the ground and soon found a place where there was no grass so I dusted it off and it looked like it opened but we couldn't open it yet so we kept on searching but first we marked that spot.

After we searched the ground of the whole clearing, we started on the walls and almost as soon as we had started we found a little notch in the wall so we tried to insert the diamond in but it didn't fit so we tried the other end and low and behold it clicked right in place.

We tried to turn it but we couldn't so we did the only thing that we could do and that was to push it down and as soon as we did we heard a rumbling and a hole opened a hole In the ceiling and water went through right where the opening was and then it clicked "waterfall" I told the others "we have to go through that hole that we marked."

We started walking towards it and we saw that the door had slid open so motioned towards Danyelle and said "after you" and she jumped in then Athero and I jumped in after her.

When we landed, we were in a pond that the waterfall led into and I looked and saw that there was a cave behind the waterfall so we started climbing out of the water and I walked around to the side of the cavern that we were in.

As we walked behind the waterfall, we soon found out that it was slick behind it because Athero fell on his tush. I helped him up, and we continued. Until we turned a corner and we ran into a rock wall.

I tested my theory, and I touched the wall and it felt smooth and I was about to pull my hand back, but I soon found myself in an unfamiliar room and then I could hear the others on the other side of the wall.

Soon I found them coming through and almost running me over and I had to get out of the way quick. Once they were through, we looked around and saw that we were in a weapons room and I saw a small box that read: first clue.

I opened it and unrolled the note and read it aloud to everyone and it said: go down the hill and up a flight of stairs, then pass through the throne room to find the hidden passage that can you can find by dethrone the king only then will you be able to complete the puzzle to get the second clue.

we went through the only door in the room and soon found that after a while the ground slanted down and I wondered after a few minutes how far down this slant went and then it leveled out and we came out into a hallway that was long enough that I couldn't see the end so we grabbed torches and walked down the hallway.

As we were walking down the hallway, I noticed that there were doors on the walls, and I knew that there had to be a flight of stairs somewhere in here.

At that very moment, we came to a halt at a rock wall and I knew that there had to be a lever or something here somewhere, so we started looking for one and finally found one after a few moments.

Athero pulled the lever and a secret door opened up in the middle of the wall.

We went through the door and found ourselves face to face with a giant staircase that was missing a couple of feet of stairs.

We looked around and soon Danyelle had found yet another mechanism and we saw it had a hole in the center of it which wasn't very high above our heads.

We started searching for the pieces for about an hour and then we found the first part of the pipe that went into the hole, so I put it into the hole.

I heard a yell and then Danyelle came running and gave me the last part of the pipe and I connected it to the other one and we all cranked the shaft until it was all the way down

Once it was all the way down, a door opened, but nothing else happened.

We went through that door and came out into that room and the first thing that we saw was an old-looking set of stone stairs.

We climbed the stairs and found ourselves in a room with a long table and at the end we saw was the king, so we pulled the chair out from underneath him and he crumbled to the ground.

We started hugging, but there was no doorway. No secret passage. Then we heard the rumbling of bones, so we looked back in time to see the king's skeleton reassembling itself.

I uncapped my blade as Athero drew his blade, and then I noticed Danyelle was backing up.

I nodded to Athero, and we lunged at the skeleton and it blocked both of our attacks and then swung his blade and we caught it with our own and then as he swung again I rolled out of the way and decapitated him and then tried to stomp on his head but before I could he grabbed it again and put it back onto his shoulders and we started again.

We did this a couple more times and then I finally got the skeleton's head under my foot but ran into another problem it would not smash.

I looked down and saw that it was no ordinary skull but one that had metal covering most of it, and that is when I noticed the fire that was lit.

I ran up; to the fire and threw the skull in and said: Hades and the head disappeared. I turned around in time to see the skeleton fall to the ground and then a door opened and we knew we had to go in.

As soon as we had passed through the door, it closed behind us and we heard a clicking sound. We turned around and could see light coming from the end of the tunnel, so we continued into the light and soon came out into this huge clearing.

We walked out, and soon we looked around. What we found in the clearing astounded all of us, and then I noticed the little town in the corner.

I walked into the town and before long I was in the center and I saw a star that had a color on each point. Then I saw a glittering out of the corner of my eye and it was red and I knew it had to be one color.

I walked up to it and saw that it was a garnet, but it was out of my reach, so I uncapped my blade and used it to push the garnet out of its mark.

I carried the garnet to the start in the town and placed it on the pedestal where the red stone had markings on. When we got to it, started glowing red along with the picture.

Then I felt a small rumble and then I saw a blue glint out of the corner of my eye in a distinct part of the clearing.

I started walking to that one and noticed that this one was even higher than the last one, so I motioned for Athero to lift me onto his shoulders so I could knock it out.

Once I got the topaz down, I picked it up and went back to the start and put it in its rightful place and like the first stone ,it glowed as well and I started noticing a beam of light coming from the stones to the center.

Then once again I felt a slight rumble and then I saw a glint of green light coming from yet another part of the clearing.

I started walking up a hill and then I noticed that it had changed direction and I knew this one was going to be tricky.

I went to it again and once again the light moved, then I started figuring out its pattern, so I went to the place where it would appear next and sure enough, it appeared right on cue.

I reached up and grabbed it before it disappeared again and raced to the star with it. I put it into the corresponding place and like the others, there was a light that went to the middle of the star and the stone lit up.

With three done and tree to go I quickly figured out that it would get harder as it went along and then I heard a buzzing sound and then I saw a white blinding light and I knew that it was another stone.

I went to it and when I went to grab it the stone got brighter. It got so bright at one point that I had to close my eyes but as soon as I grabbed it and pulled it after all the shine left the pedestal.

I walked back to the star and put the stone in the place where it needed to be and it glowed like the others, but not as bright.

I looked at the last two stone pictures and they were a signal of light and darkness, so I waited and waited but no other stones came, so we started exploring and soon we found a cave.

We went into the cave, but it wasn't big at all, so we had a look around.

Then we saw it in the corner, so we picked it up and started for the door and soon we were back at the star again with the darkness stone.

I placed it onto the dark pedestal and added its light to the others and we knew that we just had to find the light stone now.

We looked around until we saw that there was a stone hanging from the ceiling of the cave and we saw it was giving off a vast amount of light.

I picked up a rock but none of us could make it up to the rock and then I noticed that the rocks that we were throwing were giving off light as well and the one that Danyelle had just thrown had broken and was yellow inside.

I picked up another rock and broke it on the ground and when I saw it wasn't yellow in the middle. I knew that the one that Danyelle had was the one that I needed.

I went up to Danyelle, and she handed the rock to me and I cleared the rest of the dirt off of it and then walked up to the star and put the last stone in its place and the light bonded together and started moving and then it shot towards a vine-covered wall and the vines disappeared uncovering a puzzle.

We walked up to the puzzle and the first thing I did was crack my knuckles and then I got to work. I started looking around for a key and soon I had found it and when I put it into the keyhole one lever went down but there were three more to go.

So I continued searching. A few more minutes later, I had almost given up when I saw that my hand went right through the wall and so I followed that path.

What I found out was that this wall was an illusion, and then I looked around and saw that there was a key hanging on the wall of the clearing.

Then I put that key into the keyhole and the second lever went down and then I started looking for the next key.

I started going through boxes and crates that were left behind and soon I had found the next key so I went back to the keyholes and put the key into the keyhole but instead of making the third lever go down it made all of them go back up so I had to put all the keys in the keyholes again.

Then I started looking for the third key because I had found the fourth one and I started rummaging through old boxes of books and stone tablets and then I came across the third key.

I went back to the levers and put the last two keys into the last two keyholes, and the levers went down and a stone box came out of the ground.

I opened it and I picked up the note that read: go past the red and blue, but ignore through and through go past two doors and through the next and up the stairs and don't throw a fit and the third clue you shall get.

We started walking again and soon we came across a river of lava and I knew we had to cross it somehow, so we started looking for a way to cross and I saw the bridge that was half rotten.

We started looking again because we knew that this bridge wouldn't hold us. After a few minutes, I saw the lever that needed three keys to pull.

I looked around and found a cave a few meters from the river of lava, but it was quite small, so I called Athero over and pointed at the cave and asked him to go in and check to see if there was a key in there.

He got down on his hands and knees and started crawling through the small cavern and then disappeared.

A few minutes passed, then I heard a yell and then he emerged with no key in hand, so we went looking again.

I looked around and soon found another hole but this one I could fit in myself, so I went into it and after a few minutes of crawling, I saw it in front of me... the key.

It was gold with a lining of silver on it, so I picked it up and crawled back out. Then I walked up to the lever that needed the keys and put the key into the first hole, but it wouldn't fit, so I tried the second one and then finally the third.

When I tried to fit it into the third keyhole, it slid into it smoothly and then I looked around as a metal plank started rising. I kept on looking and soon I found a pile of crates that looked kind of suspicious.

I looked through them but found nothing, so I looked around again and soon found another pile, but found that had it had metal pipes.

I dug through the pipes and then one by one I lifted them up and then the last one that I lifted it up the second key fell out of and landed on the cave floor.

I picked it up and went to the second keyhole and to my surprise I had put it into the right one and then I turned my attention to find the first key as I saw the plank rise higher almost to high for the lava to pass over.

I started turning things over and then I noticed that the last key was hanging up on a hook that was above my head.

I raised my sword and pulled the key off of the hook and it slid down the blade to the hilt and I pulled it off of my sword and walked over to put the key into the first keyhole.

Then the Plank cut the river of lava off and we had a clear path to go past the river of lava. As we neared the next part of the cave, we saw a blue light up ahead.

When we walked into the next room, we noticed we were on a ledge and as we started scooting down the ledge it started getting wider until we were almost to a hidden room and in the middle of the room was a huge crack that had blue fire coming from it.

We walked up to it and I threw a rock at it and it melted on the spot and then I saw it was another three levers that would make the fire go away.

I went to the lever and then I saw the first key on the ceiling hanging over the fire and I knew I would probably have to do that one last.

I started looking around and then I noticed a chain hanging over the edge of the fire and I started touching it, but the closer I got, the hotter I got.

So I knew I had to find the third one first and then maybe that would make the fire go down enough so I could get the second key and then the first.

I started looking around and soon after a few minutes of searching, had found a possible hiding place for the third key.

I started searching the small cavern that I had found. I searched and searched but did not prevail and then I saw a metal pipe sticking out of the ground and picked it up.

When I did, I noticed it was a bar that had the shape of a key on the end and then I knew it had to be the third key, so

I went to the levers with the bar in hand and pushed it in and turned.

I pulled the lever down and the heat went down a little and I could pull the second key up from the pit and put it into the second lever and turn that one.

I heard a clunk and the first key came falling down from the ceiling and I barely caught it as it was about to fall into the pit.

Then I put that key into the first lever and pulled it down until it was all the way to the ground and then I tested it and there was no heat coming from it at all.

When I looked into it again, I noticed a lever and so I reached into the blue crack and pulled it and as soon as I did, a door opened up at the far end of the cave where there was no door before.

We went through the door and found ourselves in a long hallway that had no doors whatsoever, so we started walking and before we knew it we were at the end of the hallway.

At the end of the hall was a lever, and we tried to pull it but it wouldn't pull and then I noticed the four keyholes on the base.

I then knew that I had to find three keys in this hallway and so I started looking, but there were invisible doors so I started looking for a door that I couldn't see visually.

I started running my hand down the wall and soon I found my hand went through the wall and so I went through with it.

When I went through, I noticed I was in a much bigger room and there was a puzzle in it. I pulled Athero into the room and within a minute we had the puzzle figured out and it then revealed the first key.

We went to the lever and put the key into the first keyhole and turned and the lever blinked once and made a grinding noise and we knew it was time to find the second one.

So I started doing the same one and then I thought to myself, "maybe there is a lever in the room where we found the first key." I went back to that room and sure enough, there in the corner was a lever like the one that we needed the keys for.

I pulled it, and as soon as I did, I heard the grinding of gears. When I went into the hallway, I noticed that there were tiny openings in the wall, so I went into the first one and found a similar puzzle.

I called Athero over and soon he had that puzzle figured out almost as soon as he got there. Then, as soon as he got the puzzle figured out, a door opened, and a key was on the ground.

I picked it up and went to the lever and put the second key into it and we heard saw the lever flash twice and then it made a buzzing noise again and soon we were looking for the third and final key and so we went into the next tiny door and saw that there was another puzzle however this one was a little different.

When Athero tried to do the puzzle the way he did the others it didn't work so he tried to do several other ways and then he noticed the hammer and bells.

We went up to it and I noticed that there was flaps on the puzzle and I hit the first bill with the hammer and the first flap opened and then he hit the third one and they all closed and then we had to start all over so once again I hit the first one and it opened and then he hit the second one and it closed again.

We did it a few more times and then we finally got it and in front of us appeared the key, so I went back to the keyhole.

With the key in, the door opened, and we saw three doors in front of us, so we went past the first two and went through the third one.

When we went through it we came out onto a staircase and we went through the door at the top of the stairs and saw a box in the middle of the room so I walked up to it and opened it and it read: go past this room and down the hall but do not stall or you will have to answer the call, go past the crystals of fire and ice, go past the table with the bountiful feast, do the keys and you'll get the first shield piece.

We walked out the door and soon I found I was out in a hallway that was lined with doors and I knew we had to stay in the hall and not pick any doors.

As we were walking down the hall, we saw the doors began disappearing and then as soon when we were at the end of the hallway; we saw there was a door in front of us.

So we went through it only to find ourselves in a room that had a waterfall in the center and a lake that it ran into.

We walked past the waterfall and went into the next room, that was filled to the brim with old bronze swords.

We started going through it trying to find a door and then I noticed the door was at the far end of the room so we climbed down and started for the door, but as soon as we got close, we found it sealed.

I looked around and saw a switch on the opposite side of the room and so I went to it and pulled it and it unlocked the door and I knew that someone had to stay at the switch and keep the door open but when Athero went to it; the door locked itself again.

So I started searching for the switch and discovered that it had to have a pin that would go into the bottom of the switch, so I started searching for one and soon found a box in a corner that might have it.

I opened the box and found out that it was the pin and it was golden and long, so I picked it up and put it into the hole in the switch and it fit snugly.

We walked up to the door slowly, and it started shutting, but then it slowed down and stopped and we went through it and found ourselves in another hallway; but this one was lit with torches by magic.

We walked down this hall and soon we walked up to a door and we went through it into a room that was lit with fire red crystals and Athero started walking close but I pulled him back because I knew that something would happen if you touched them.

I inspected the crystals and soon I found my arm reaching up and I had to have Athero pull me back and we started moving again and when we left that room; we went into another hallway.

We walked down the hall and after a while we came to a door that we went through and when we did; I saw we were in another room that was filled to the brim with bronze shields.

Before I looked around in the pile of shields, I looked for a door, but all I saw was a pile of boxes. So I started looking through the shields and that is when I thought that there might be a switch behind the boxes.

I climbed down and started moving boxes, and surprisingly, to see that I was right. As soon as I finished moving the boxes, I saw that the lever-like switch also needed a pin, but I didn't know where to look this time because there were no more boxes.

So I started looking for a mirage wall and soon I found it on the far wall and I went through it in a jiffy and there in the mirage room was a single box and a lever so before I went to the box I went to the lever but it didn't move.

So I went to the box and opened it and inside was a silver pin, so I went to the switch in the treasure room and started looking for a place to put it but couldn't find one.

Then it clicked "I had to put it in the lever in the mirage room". Then I went to the mirage room and started looking over that lever and saw a tiny hole in the base.

When I put it in I heard a clunk and then I pulled it and heard a whooshing sound and I saw the switch by the outer wall light up so I went to it and pulled it to find that it opened a door next to it.

We went through the door and found ourselves in a room with ice blue crystals that were almost identical to the red ones except the color.

We walked through that room fast because we knew that if we stayed, we would get drawn to the crystals and something bad would happen.

We went through the door to the far end of the room and came out into the living room. On the table was an enchanted feast to last forever, and we saw a door on the other side of the table and so we went through it into a smaller room that had a puzzle.

I went up to it and saw that it needed three keys, one on the left and right and one on the front. We started looking for a secret room but found a secret passageway, so we went through it and on the other side was a lever.

I pulled the lever, and it made a buzzing sound and I knew that I had uncovered something. So I went back through the passage back to the bigger room and I immediately knew what I had uncovered.

There was a wall that was there but now wasn't. I went into the room that was beyond that wall and started having a look around, then I motioned for the others to follow me.

I finally found the first key, and I went to put it into the keyhole and turned and the key started going inside it until only the handle was showing.

I went back to the room and started looking again, but I couldn't find anything except cobwebs and dust on everything and then I noticed that there was a puzzle uncovered in the main room and in the side room.

So I pulled Danyelle and Athero over and they got to work on the one in the main room as I got to work on the one in the side room.

After a few minutes of working hard, I just started getting irritated, and I was about to quit until I started figuring it out. I looked at the floor and saw shapes and I stepped on one and it lit up, so I stepped on another and the first one had stopped.

So I did it again and this time I stepped on the other one and they both lit up and then I stepped on the third one and they all three lit up and the puzzle shimmered and the lever started glowing.

I looked up to see Danyelle and Athero walking up and so I pulled the lever, but I had to do it with their help because it seemed to be stuck and it clicked into place and showed a key.

I picked up the key and went back to the lever and put it in and it buzzed as it pulled the last key into place and the lever started glowing, so we pulled it down and it turned with us on it.

When it stopped, we saw we were in an unfamiliar room and in front of us was an ancient box. We walked up to it and inside was half of the handle of the shield.

Athero pulled out a map and said, "the next place we need to go is the temple of the Olympian Zeus."

I pulled out a teleportation marble and rolled it and we thought of where we needed to go and it made a portal and when we went through to another part of Greece, the weather changed because we were outside again.

CHAPTER 3

TEMPLE OF THE OLYMPIAN ZEUS

As s we entered the temple of the Olympian Zeus (which took up a good acre or two of land) we noticed that there wasn't hardly anything left of it so we started looking for the same glyph that had sucked us into the cavern last time and soon found it on the statue base.

This time I walked up to it and asked if Danyelle wanted to do the honors and she walked up to it and activated it and then one by one we all touched it and got sucked into the cave below.

When we landed, we landed in water, but by the time I had landed, the others were already on shore waiting on me by the water.

Once I got onto the shore we started looking around and soon the note started forming on the wall and it said: "go out the door carved into the wall and ignore the roars and past the waterfall down the steps and up another down a slope without a blunder and you'll come out alive and you will find the note that will lead you to clue one of five ."

We started looking around for a door that was etched into the wall like it said but couldn't find any and that is when I tripped a rock and a lever came out of the wall.

I went up to the lever and pushed it down and then I heard a rumbling coming from the wall next to me, so I went to investigate. What I found was a door that was not there before.

I motioned for the others to follow me through the door and so we started walking and then we started hearing growls and roars coming from all directions, so we just kept in mind what the note said.

We began inching forward and soon we started going up and then we came to a clearing that had a waterfall at the far end that was huge and I knew we had to go past it. Then, as we neared the waterfall, I saw a door behind it and as I neared it, the doors behind the waterfall; they opened to reveal a set of stairs that were leading down.

We started going down the stairs and soon we were in another hallway and in the hallway was another stairway, but this one was going up.

We started going up the stairs and soon we were on level ground that we couldn't see the end of, so we kept on walking and soon the levelness of the ground began sloping down to a factor that we could barely walk down it.

When we finally got down to the end of the slope, I almost tripped over a line and I would have died if Athero hadn't pulled me back in time.

If I had been there, I would have sliced in two because a giant ax came out of the wall. Once I saw the line, I cut it and we passed it and I saw holes in the walls and I knew things would shoot out of them.

I told the others "watch where you step ok?" They just looked at me and nodded and we picked our steps carefully and then Danyelle picked a very unwise step and an arrow shot out and barely missed her.

I pulled her straight, and she thanked me and we continued on our way until we were at the very end and at the other end in front of us was a gold box with Zeus painted on the front of it.

I opened the box and read to the others "past the birds of old and the paintings that happened long ago, down this hall and pick right between a sword or a bow and you'll find the clue one of five once you pass the lava and the emeralds, stay warm in the cold.

We started walking again and soon we were in this big open area that had a lot of archaeopteryxes in it and I instantly knew that they were the birds of old that it was talking about.

We started having a look around because these birds were supposed to be extinct, yet here they were in a proper environment, happy and alive.

We started moving again and after a while we found the door to the hallway that led to the next room and we started going into the hallway and after a while we came out into the next room.

When we got to the next room, what we saw was it filled with cave drawings and we started looking them over and soon we saw an arrow that was pointing towards a painting that showed the gods rising from the depths of the earth.

Then we noticed the second painting that symbolizes one god separating from the others and then the one after that it symbolized the splitting of the different gods.

Then we noticed the door at the far end of the room and we went through it into the next room that was empty except for a wooden sword and a golden bow and I saw the others immediately going for the bow but I said "no...it's a test...gold would be more but the sword is a much better weapon and we picked up the sword and immediately a light shone on it and made it a real sword".

The door at the other end unlocked. We went through it, leaving the sword behind. We entered the next room.

In the middle of the room was a big emerald and as I was looking at it I felt drawn to and before I knew it I was reaching out to touch it and Danyelle had to pull me back and she said to the others "we better get out of this room as fast as we can".

They covered my eyes and started walking me towards the door, but the door had disappeared and so we started looking for another one.

After minutes of panicking, I finally found a button, but all that did was make a clicking sound that sounded like someone starting a fire.

Then they let go of me and I walked to the wall and into a hallway and then I heard the others calling my name and

I said, "I'm in the hallway, it's a mirage hallway...just feel the wall".

I saw them touch the wall but keep their distance from the emeralds and then they fell into me and we started walking again until we could see a bright red light and when we walked into the next room; we saw that in the middle of the room was a river of lava.

There in the center of the room was a lever with four keys and saw the room filled with puzzles.

I went to work on the first one and soon I was having difficulty with it, so Danyelle stepped over to me and started working on it with me and soon we had it all figured out.

Then we moved to the next one, and we had even more difficulty even with the two of us working on it, but eventually we got it all figured out, so we started working on the third one.

Now this one had a combination of many things that you had to figure out, but we worked on it and then Athero came to help and with all three of us working on it, we got it.

Then we got to working on the fourth and final one, but this one was actually the

easiest one out of the three and we got it down pretty fast and when we got done, a key came out of the ground and I saw the key and put it in the lever and as soon as I did part of the lever lit up.

I started searching for the remaining three keys and soon found the second one and I gave it to Danyelle to put in the lever and when she did, the second part of the lever lit up.

Then I started looking for the third one and as soon as I started looking I had found it in a few wooden crates and I gave this one to Athero and he put it in the third keyhole and the third part of the lever lit up.

I just started looking when Danyelle said "found it" and put it into the last keyhole and the rest of the lever lit up and the lever went down and pulled up a blockage that wouldn't let any lava through.

So we walked across and then as we were stepping on the opposite bank, the lava began overflowing and then the dam that we had put up had burst and lava started going everywhere.

On the opposite wall was a box that was silver but other than that there was no description on it so I opened the lid and inside was a note that read past the doors with the blood red look, past the big stone giant rock up the slope and down the hill and find the note to the number two clue".

We started walking again and after a while we found this room that led in three directions so we tried the left one but it only went to the right one and so we went through the center and hit a brick wall.

I touched it to see if I would get sucked through, but no such luck so we doubled back and went to have another look around and personally, I'm glad we did because we had missed a hallway.

We started walking down this hallway and immediately knew that we were in the first part of the note: the hallway with the blood red doors. Moments of climbing the stairs, we reached the top, and I looked at the color of the stairs and saw that it was blood red.

We started down the hallway that was in front of us and after an hour of walking down that hallway and soon we were standing in front of an enormous boulder and we just barely squeezed past it.

Almost as soon as we passed the first one, another giant rock blocked our path, and we saw we could not get around it.

We started looking around for a way to get the rock out of the way and were about to give up when Danyelle found a two by four in a hidden part of the wall and I got up and said, "that will work nicely".

We wedged the board under the rock and it rolled away into the same hidden room and we started walking again. Soon as we were walking again.

After a few more moments of walking, we started going downhill, and I noticed we had to be on the slope that it mentioned in the note.

We kept going down for a while and after an hour or two; I began wondering when were we going uphill again or at least level out.

We walked for two more minutes and then finally it leveled out and then we were staring at another hallway. We started walking down the hall and soon we were going through the door at the other end of the hall.

On the other side of the door was a hill and so we started climbing, but we and then suddenly we were at the top of the hill and we went down.

It took just as long to get to the foot of the hill, but what we found at the end of the hill was an old building and the box to the second clue was nowhere to be seen.

We knew it had to be in the building, so we opened the doors, which nearly fell on us by the way, and started looking for the box that would hold the second clue.

All that we could find was a pedestal that was holding an ancient book, so we moved the book and started searching the pedestal and in the process ended up knocking it over.

When the dust cleared, we saw it had the clue in a hole that the pedestal was covering.

I went into the hole to get the box and when I got out, we all gathered around the box. I opened the box and inside was a tablet that read: through the gates, past the pillars of fire and through the fog with an admirer take a left then a right then you shall get to the third note that tells the due and you shall find the third clue.

We started walking again and soon we got to yet another hallway and as we were walking down it we felt a brief rumble and I knew we had to be way down deep into the earth's crust.

We finished walking down the hall and soon we came upon a gold gate, but when I touched it, the dang thing shocked the heck out of me.

I looked at it and saw that it had a picture of a satire on it so I took a few minutes of thinking, then it clicked.

I motioned for Danyelle to open the gate and to no one's surprise; it didn't shock her and it opened right away. We went through the gate and started walking again, and soon we were in a giant cave that had a giant lava lake in the middle.

We walked into the cave and the first thing that we saw was a bright orange twister made of fire whirling around in the lava lake.

We saw the door on the other side of the cave, but some bushes blocked it.

We tried to go through the bushes but they came alive and when they did; I started getting so angry that lightning was coming out of my hands and then suddenly; the bushes caught fire.

The bushes started running every which way and we took this moment to go through the exit. Once we were through the doors, we were in darkness and so we started feeling the walls.

Then a light came on, but we didn't know where the light was coming from until I noticed the lightning bugs near the ceiling of the hall.

We continued walking now that we had light and after a few minutes; the hall took a left turn and continued. We pressed on and then the hallway took a right, then came out into another cave.

We saw that there was a lever at the far end of the room. I walked up to it and saw that it was a complicated lever.

I studied it and started onto it and after a few moments I got the first part of the lever figured out and then a few moments later I got the second part figured out and then the third.

After I got the lever figured out, I heard a click and then I knew I could pull it, so when I went to pull it and to my amazement it went down extremely easily.

When I pulled the lever, a part of the wall gave way, leaving a misty pathway, and I knew it had to be the last part.

We started into the mist and grabbed each other's hands so we wouldn't lose each other. I led the way down the hall, then it split in two and I thought it would be a trick, so I had a look around.

I pulled them past the halls and soon found one in a place hidden by mist. We went up that hallway and past several doors and past a staircase and then down one and then the hallway started curving to the left and then took a sharp left.

After a while of walking down that hall, it came to a "t" and then we took the right one and after a few moments, it curved to the right.

As we followed it, the walls changed from gray to red and then to black, and I knew we were getting close to the second clue.

We walked for a few more minutes and then we came out into this clearing and in the middle of the clearing was a waterfall and I guessed that the second clue to the second piece was behind it.

I began walking towards it and I had just realized exactly how far it was to the waterfall.

When I finally made it to the waterfall, it seemed to want to part so I could go through without getting wet.

I went through the waterfall and inside was a chest that was made of wood. I walked up to it, opened the chest, and found it filled with gold; then we searched for a box to hold the second clue.

We looked everywhere and then I looked up and noticed that it had an attic and we didn't notice the stairs.

I went up the stairs and immediately I saw the gold box and I knew it had the clue in it.

I picked it and dropped it down to Danyelle and Athero, then I climbed back down.

Once I was down, I opened the box and we all peered inside and I picked up the clue inside.

I made sure everyone was listening and then I read: go through the door to the far end of the room down the hall and past the giants made of rock past the green red and blue and past the enormous moving waterfall and you'll find the second note.

I looked up and, like the clue said, there was a door. We went through that door and started walking down this long hallway and before we knew it; we were in yet another large cave.

I started looking around, and soon I discovered some stone trees that were huge. Then I noticed it was the trees that were the stone giants.

I saw that there was a door in one of them and it was against the wall of the cave so I walked through the door and soon I found myself in a fork that had a ruby above one door, a sapphire above another, and an emerald on the last.

I went for the emerald one first, but it came up to be a dud. Next I did the ruby, and it also came up to be a dud, so I knew it had to be the last one.

I went into the last one but to my surprise it was also a dud. Then I noticed the door hidden in shadow in the corner and I went to it and opened it and on the other side was a field that had the most beautiful waterfall.

I went up to the waterfall, and I noticed it was swaying and I saw a door to the far end of the field.

I walked to the door at the far end of the field and went into a hallway that led to a small room with one other door and inside the room was a small wooden box that had a small paper in it.

I waited for the others to gather around me and then I read: go past the river of lava and the river of ice. Go past the pillar of fire and the ice tornado and go past the frozen mushrooms and then thou shalt get the third clue.

We started walking, and we came to a door and there was no handle but the lightning bolt engraving gave me an idea.

I gathered up my energy and hoped that it would work and pushed the door and to my surprise it opened, revealing a red light illuminating from the walls ahead.

We walked inside and the first thing I noticed was the large river of lava flowing slowly through the middle of the room.

I started looking for a lever that would block the lava and saw it in the corner with four keyholes in it.

I started looking for the first key and that is when I noticed the holes in the walls, so I went to one and saw that they were not too deep.

I reached my hand into one and it grabbed onto something metal and so I pulled my hand back out and in my hand was the first key.

I went to the lever and put the first key into the lever, and it flashed. Then I went to look for the second key. I was about to give up when I noticed a shine out of the corner of my eye.

I turned my head and saw that the second key was in the lava, so I had to be very careful not to burn myself.

I hooked the key around the handle and pulled it out of the lava and I put the second key into the lever and it flashed twice.

Then I went looking for the third key but before I could find it Danyelle passed it to me and I put it into the lever and it flashed three times and then I got to looking for the last one.

Before I could find this one, Athero found it in a pile of boxes and he gave it to me so I went over to it and the lever flashed four times, then the lever started going down all by itself.

As it was going down, the lava was getting cut off by a double enforced steel blockage. We walked through where the lava used to be and we went to the other side.

We went through the door on the other side and started in the next room, where there was an ice river that we had to cross.

We walked up to the river, and I tried to cross but I fell through and came out on the other side so I just told the others to just swim across then Danyelle said "my kind can't swim so if you have any suggestions I'm all ears."

Athero stepped forward and said, "I can carry her across" I nodded. Once we were all across, I walked up to the only door to the exit and I saw it had a puzzle that we had to solve and it was a three-part puzzle.

I worked on the middle puzzle as the others worked on the others. After a few minutes had passed, I had my puzzle figured out and then I noticed the others were already done.

When I got done, the lock clicked off, and the door opened, revealing a large room with a large swirling red fire pillar going around the middle of the room.

I entered the room and nearly got sucked up and I knew that we would have to do this part rather slowly so we inched little by little past the pillar of fire and as we neared the exit, I almost got blown away again but I grabbed a column and centered myself again.

Then I started again. Once we had got through that, we closed that door behind us and started off again.

We came out into a hallway and after a few hours in the hallway; we came out in another room and this one was even more windy and that is when we noticed the ice twister.

We inched our way against the wall because the twister was throwing ice shards everywhere.

I was almost to the door when an ice shard blocked my path and I had to backtrack. So I started itching to the other side and after a few minutes I finally made it to the door and as soon as I had made it through the door an ice shard came flying at where I was a second ago.

Because of the ice shards, Danyelle and Athero were delayed by an hour and a half. Closing the door behind us banished the wind.

We started walking and soon we were walking along another hallway lined with glowing mushrooms, so I knew we were on the right track.

We went down one hallway and through another, and then we were in an immense room that was colder than the other rooms.

Inside were some frozen mushrooms that were as thick as trees and so frozen that they had turned white and they towered over us, almost hitting the ceiling.

We started looking for the door and soon found it after about a few hours of looking. It was at the far end of the room in the dark.

We went through the door into a hallway that was also lined with mushrooms and we walked down that hallway to the next room.

In the next room there was a puzzle and it had a sign that read :beat the puzzle and win the prize.

We lined up the images and shapes on the pedestal and puzzle and part of the wall crumbled down revealing the third box clue.

I bent down and opened the box and picked up the clue and read :past the statues of Hera and ran into the golden room. Move the pedestal and illuminate the room.

We went through the doors at the other end of the room and soon we were walking down another hallway that led forward for a while.

After; about an hour we came to some statues, and i knew they were the statues of Hera and Zeus and we just walked right past them.

We kept on walking as fast as we could and soon we could see a light coming from up ahead.

When we stepped through the door that was making the light, we noticed we were in a room made entirely out of gold.

Other than the room was golden, it was like any other room. So we just moved forward and went into the next hallway and soon we found ourselves in a room that wasn't as big as the others that we have been in.

We looked around and the first thing I saw was the fact that this room had a pedestal in the center, so I went up to it and tried to move it, but it wouldn't budge.

Then I looked at the side and I saw it required a key and so I began looking all over the room for a key that would probably be silver.

I started searching the walls and soon I found the secret room and the place for the key was there but no key, so I started looking again and saw it in a corner blending in with the wall.

I picked up the key and put it into the pedestal and the pedestal rolled aside, revealing a mirror.

We left that room and soon we were in a hallway that had black walls and I rubbed my finger on it and smelled my finger and I knew it was lead.

Then I looked around and saw the chains and dead bodies in cages and then I saw the note.

I picked it up and opened it and then motioned for the others to come over to me and as soon as they were over with me; I picked it out of the box and started reading.

Go down the hall, past the waterfall and field, through the locked door. After this clue, there is no more. Continue past the lava and crystals and diamonds; some climbing will be required to reach your last clue.

We went through the door at the far end of the room and down the hallway until we came to a door that opened up into a field that had a waterfall and at the opposite side of the field I could see a door but it looked like it was closed.

We walked across the field, past the waterfall, and stopped in front of the door. I saw the door sealed, and it proved to be a puzzle gate.

I used the panel to move the shapes back and forth into the right sequence until I heard a click, but there was only one click and there were three locks, so I had to unlock the other two.

That is when I looked over the puzzle and the panel. The puzzle had a hole in it where something round could go, and the panel had three keys to go with it .

So I started looking for the pole first and after about thirty minutes, I found it. I dug it up and cleaned it up a little and then brought it to the puzzle and put it in, and it fit perfectly.

I pushed it and I heard another click and I knew that I just needed to find the keys now. I started searching again, but this time for keys.

After a few minutes, I found the first key, and I walked over to the panel and put the key in, and turned. I started searching again and after a few minutes, my electricity started going haywire and I knew it was leading me to it.

I reached out my hand and electricity shot out of my hand and showed me where the next key was. I picked it up and put it into the panel and turned it.

I put my hand out again but this time it did nothing so I started searching and then suddenly it fired up again so I put out my hand again and this time electricity showed me where the last key was.

I went to it, picked it up and put it in the panel and turned it and all the keys sank into the panel and the door unlatched and swung open.

I went through the door and found myself in a big room that had a river of lava going through it and there was a lever on its bank.

I motioned for the others to help me find the keys to the lever, then I started looking and soon I found the first key and I put it into the lever and turned.

I heard the grinding of gears and I knew it had worked and we only had to find two more.

I went back to searching and soon I had found key number two and I put that key into the lever and turned and I heard the grinding of gears again and so I just needed to find one more key.

I didn't even have to search for the last key because it was in plain sight, so I went and picked it up and put it into the lever and the lever went down, making the lava stop flowing so we could cross.

We walked across the ground that a few minutes ago was lava, and then we went through the door and landed ourselves in yet another hallway.

We started walking and soon we came to a cave that had a lot of diamonds on the walls. We walked past those and came to a large chasm.

I started looking around and at first I thought of the vines that were hanging from the ceiling, but I decided against it.

Then I saw the ledge, but I didn't see any way to get up to it and so I kept on looking and soon I found a rock wall and I started preparing myself to climb it.

I took the first step but screwed something up because I fell almost immediately, so I tried a different approach.

I used the lowest ledge to help pull me up, and I was almost there until the ledge piece I was holding onto broke off and I fell again.

I thought and decided that there had to be a different way, so I started scanning the room and that is when I noticed the vine wall that went from wall to wall.

I climbed onto the vine wall and started inching my way across the room, and little by little I was getting there.

Then the vine that my left hand had a hold of broke and I barely managed staying on the wall. I grabbed another vine and continued to inch my way across.

The vines I had a hold of broke a couple more times and I just grabbed a new one and kept on inching my way across.

Once I got about halfway across, I saw that there was a ledge below me, so I got on that instead, inching, but that was almost instantly shut down because as soon as I had laid my foot on it, it crumbled.

I got back on the vine and started inching across the room again. After; a few minutes of inching, I finally made it to the side with Athero by my side and then I noticed we had left Danyelle behind.

I looked around and noticed a lever in the corner and decided I had nothing to lose, so I pulled it and it made discs appear in midair.

Danyelle jumped onto them and then onto the side that we were on and then we progressed and we went through the doors in front of us.

When we got through the doors, we saw we were in an enormous room filled with many things, from gold to jewels and even pots of flour. Then my line of sight was captivated by the box that was in the corner.

I went over to it and motioned for the others to come over to me so I could read it to them.

Once they were with me, I opened the box and read the paper and it said: this is the note that will tell you where to find the last clue for this piece. Go past the everlasting fire and the never ceasing water, go through the gate of kind souls and you shall get the note to the last clue.

We started walking for a while and we went from one room to another until we made it back to where we started from.

We took another door and went down that hallway and found ourselves in a hallway and we just kept on walking and then came out into a room that very well could have been a throne room.

We moved the throne away from the wall and, as usual, there was a passageway behind it. We got on our hands and knees and began crawling through that tunnel and after a few minutes of doing so; came out into a beautiful room.

We entered the room and found it filled with beautiful paintings portraying the everlasting fire, and it was in a pot of some sort. Then I noticed the pot in the center of the room and I saw it was the same pot that was being portrayed in the pictures.

Without thinking, I went up to the pot and grabbed a torch off the wall and put the torch under the pot but it wouldn't light so I put the torch on top of the pot and it blazed to life like no other and when it did; I heard a low rumbling and saw a door open at the far end of the room.

We went through that door and went down the hall and went into another room that was also huge but this one was a little different because it had two chests.

We went to the chest on the right first and it opened easily but there wasn't anything in it, so I went to the one on the left and in it was a button.

I pushed the button, and I heard a click and then a large waterfall starting and I knew it had to be the everlasting water, but was I ever in for a surprise?

Right after it had started, it had stopped, and a ladder appeared to go inside the waterfall hole, so I climbed the ladder and soon I saw another button and so I pushed it.

I heard the roaring of water as soon as I did and when I got back out; I looked around, and I saw a big waterfall that was more huge than the last.

I looked around and saw a button at the base of the waterfall and I knew it would open the next place up for us.

I pushed it and I felt a low humming and a door began opening up and I began walking up to it and I went through it along with my friends.

We went down the dark hallway until we came into a room that was a little smaller than the others but still a pretty good size and I was the door that had a symbol of a soul on it so I knew we had to go through that door.

The only thing was there was no way to open it. Then I saw the giant keyhole in the center, but a key that big we easily can find, so why was it nowhere in sight?

Then it became clear {I had to build it}.

I walked up to the door and counted all the spaces that would need a piece and I counted six pieces, so I started looking and found one right away in a barrel near the entrance.

Then I started looking for the second piece and after a good few minutes of looking, I found it lying on a crate and I hooked them together.

Making half the handle, then I started looking again and soon found the third piece in a vase and I connected that one to the other two and saw that the handle was almost done.

I started looking for the fourth piece and after an hour of hard searching I finally found it in the bottom of a water barrel and then I hooked that one to the others and I saw I had the handle and now all I needed was the key part and the part that connects the handle to the key part.

I started looking for the fifth piece and after a few moments I could find it by the doorway and then I connected that piece to the others and started looking for the last piece.

I searched for a good few hours for the last piece and when I found it, I felt stupid because it was right in front of my face the entire time.

I picked it up and connected it to the others and saw that I now had a key in my hand, so I went to the door and put the key into it and turned and it creaked open.

On; the other side of the door was a device that looked like it came out of a sixties movie and I knew I had to walk through it to the other side.

I walked up to it and immediately the machine turned itself on and I walked through it and as I did; I felt weird and then the feeling was gone.

When I was done, I turned around to see Athero glowing with energy as he passed through, and the same thing happened to Danyelle.

Once we were through the gates of souls, we saw the box rise from a hole in the ground that was just uncovered.

We walked up to it and I looked at the others and they just nodded and smiled. I opened the lid and inside was a note that read: down the hall and in the next room you'll find the key that will either save you or lead you to your doom, you'll have to look far and wide and also who you are inside to get the next shield piece.

We went walking and went through a door to the left and went down the hall and took the first door into a giant room. I pointed to Danyelle and said, "you take that part, I'll take this part". Then I turned to Atheros and said, "and you take over there; we will meet in the middle." With that, we started searching the room, but we found nothing.

That was until I moved some boxes and uncovered a moveable tile and found a key that had a key on each side, so I guessed one side would get us the piece and one side would send us to our doom.

So I studied it and soon I noticed a skull on one side and a lightning bolt on the other and I knew which side to use.

We started looking for the door that the key went to, but there was no door that looked like it would house the key anywhere in sight.

We went into the next room and then the room after that and checked all the rooms in the hall, but none looked like it housed that key, so we started digging a little into this key.

What we found was that the key doesn't go to a door, it goes to a cabinet in the main room.

We went back the way we came and finally got back to the main room where the bed and sleeping chambers were.

We started going through the room and started searching for a cabinet because there wasn't one attached to the wall.

After a while, I was the only one still searching because Athero and Danyelle had got tired. I searched under the bed and in the belongings and then after a long time I finally found a cabinet but turns out it was the wrong one.

So I started searching again and after a few hours I was about to give up and then I saw the corner of the room, and in the shadows a black cabinet that was about as tall as I was and as wide as a horse with frills and designs all over it.

We got into it and to our surprise; it fit all of us with plenty of room for about two more and then we closed the door and locked it from the inside.

Then we heard a bump coming from outside and we quickly unlocked the cabinet and we all filed out. In front of us was the box that the next shield piece was in.

I opened it and inside was the second part of the arm piece and so I put it with the other one and when I put it in my bag, I heard a clunk and I pulled it out again and I saw it had fuzed with the first piece so I just thought "cool" and put it back in my bag.

Then Athero pulled out the map, and I asked, "where do we go next?" He answered "the temple of Zeus".

I asked "again" and he said "different from I expected." So I rolled the marble and thought of where we needed to go and a portal appeared and we went through it back to Greece, where it was a nice day.

THE TEMPLE OF ZEUS

When we got there, I noticed this temple looked a lot different from the last one and we started looking around so that we could find the glyph that would take us underground.

Then I heard a yell and I'm guessing that Athero heard it as well, because we both came running just in time to see Danyelle get sucked into the glyph.

We hurried and touched the glyph before it went away and got sucked in as well and when we landed; we landed on a lot of stalks. So we crawled off the stalks and found ourselves face to face with a wall, and letters were forming on the wall.

It read: as a note goes past the gold, up the ladder and down the swell,lope by the ledge, that'll do and you'll find the first clue.

We went through the door to the right and went into another room that was filled with silver but not gold so we went through the door to the next room and found this room filled to the brim with jewels so we went through the door to the next room.

As we entered the next room, we noticed it had gold bricks to the ceiling, and we knew that the first part of the note meant this room.

Then I noticed the door out of the room and I motioned for the others to follow me and I went through the door and, to my surprise, it led to a hallway.

We started walking and soon the hallway started curving to the left and then I almost ran onto a golden ladder and I stopped just in time.

I started climbing the ladder into the darkness and then I came into the lit up cave and as we came out we saw we were in a bigger cave than before.

When I was fully out, I helped the others get off the ladder and then I had a look around and soon; I had found a switch. I asked "Danyelle do you want to do the honors"?

She nodded and came over but she couldn't pull it down so I tried to help her but I was no help because even with our combined strength we couldn't bring it down, so we all pulled at once and it crept.

When we had got it pulled all the way down, we noticed that there was a door that wasn't there before and it was closing fast, so we ran through it and we had barely got through it before it closed on us.

When we went through, we began having a look around and I saw we were in a corridor so we started walking and after a few moments of walking; we started feeling the slope going down.

We went down for a few minutes and then we started slipping and then soon we were falling into the darkness.

When we finally landed, we were at a ledge and on the other side was the clue that we needed to get to.

I sat down and threw a rock across the chasm and the rock just floated in midair sitting on something, so I put my eye close to the ground and looked across the chasm and the thing I saw astonished me.

When I looked across, I saw a road that went across the chasm and it blended itself into the wall so the person would think that there wasn't anything there.

I got up and started walking toward the edge and as I went to walk off the edge; the others went crazy and started trying to pull me back.

I turned to them and told them to look at the ground and they'd see what I'm doing. When they did, they stopped trying to pull me back.

Instead, they urged me forward, so I went walking up to the edge and walked off to find myself walk into thin air and I just kept walking until I was on the other side.

Once I was on the other side, I waited for the others to get onto the other side and when they finally did; they congratulated me on finding the way across.

We started going to the chest that would have the clue and I opened it and inside was a little piece of paper that had some writing on it that read: go past the silver statues and down the winding tunnel and before you can enter through the hidden passage; you will have to complete the puzzle and you shall find the note for the second clue.

Then I heard a rumbling sound, and I turned to see a door opening and we rushed through a hallway that was lined with pictures and then up ahead we could see the two gleaming statues shining like the sun.

As we got closer, we saw they were just mirages; the real statues were farther ahead. We started walking down the hall and soon we came across some more statues, but as we got closer to them, they also turned out to be mirages.

This happened a few more times and then after an hour of this we saw two statues, one of Hera and one of Zeus, and we knew that these had to be the real ones.

We walked up to them and sure enough they were the real statues (u could tell because they didn't disappear when we got close) and we started walking again and soon we came across a crossway.

I chose the left one, and they all followed me into it and at the end we saw it branched into three again, so I let Danyelle choose and she chose the right one.

When we got through there, we passed a sign that said "the winding tunnel". We went into the tunnel that was the winding tunnel and soon it started moving like a snake.

As we were going down that tunnel, I starting feeling sick to my stomach and soon I had to hold on to the walls for support but that wasn't helping.

After a while, we began seeing the light at the end of the tunnel appear and disappear every few moments, and that made me feel a lot better.

As we made our way to the end of the winding tunnel, I made a discovery and that is that the walls were of granite and they were quickly deteriorating and I was ready to be out of here.

At that moment, we came out into the tunnels that we were in before and we just started walking again down the hall.

All we needed to do now is look for the puzzle and then go find the hidden passage. Soon we were in a hallway with doors on the sides.

There were three doors on the left side and two on the right. I told Danyelle to check the right side while I checked the left.

After I got done checking the left doors, I went looking for Danyelle because she was nowhere to be seen and Athero and I started opening doors on the right side and soon found her fighting a man eating plant.

I uncapped my marker sword and cut the stupid thing in quarters and she just stood there with her arms crossed and said, "I had it". Then I noticed the puzzle behind her.

Then I said to her "you've found it" but the puzzle was already done and then I figured it out. The puzzle was to kill the beast and in that moment a door opened and we went through it and found ourselves on the hidden passage and we followed that for a while and then after a few backtracks and breaks we started walking a while until we came across that lever.

I pulled the lever and soon I could see the wall lifting until we could see a piece of paper just lying there on the ground so I had Danyelle pick it up and it read: go past the river of lava and hot water, past the picture of the dead man's daughter, up the hill and down the slope but not without lots of hope and you'll find the second clue, now go on for that'll do.

We started walking and pretty soon we came to a river that looked like a regular river but as I threw a leaf in it burned up into ashes in seconds.

Then I saw the lever, and I motioned for the others to follow me and I started pulling the lever down, but to no avail. Then I started looking it over and saw that it needed three keys.

I started turning over crates and barrels and after the fourth batch of barrels that I turned over I found the first key. I went back to the lever and put the first key into the keyhole and turned.

I heard the familiar grinding and saw a blockage start to rise but it only rose a few feet and then I turned my gaze onto looking for the second key.

I looked in vases and under bags and then I heard Danyelle say" found one" and she came over and gave it to me (seriously I don't know why they keep giving them to me).

I put the key into the keyhole and turned this one too and again I heard the grinding and the barricade rose higher.

Then not even ten minutes later I heard Danyelle and Athero both yell out "found one" and once again they gave the keys to me so I went to the lever and put the keys into the keyholes and one by one I turned them and the water stopped flowing but it wouldn't for long.

We crossed the river in a hurry and almost as soon as we were across; the barricade broke, and the water came crashing down and we hurried into the next room where there was a lava river waiting for us.

I knew that we would have to find more keys. I was right; there were six keys that needed to be found this time.

I started looking under everything and then I heard them calling my name and I knew I must have found a secret room. I walked out and waved for them to follow, and then I went back into the room and started looking for the first key.

You can imagine my surprise when I moved a rug and the first key was under it half buried in sand, so I picked it up and was about to be stung by a scorpion.

I put the first key into the lever and turned and then the metal barricade went up a little and I went back to looking for the keys.

After; an hour of looking, I found another key right, as Danyelle also did. She brought hers to me and I put both of them into the lever and turned them.

When I did, the barricade moved up a few more inches and was barely below the surface.

Then, Athero told me;"I've got another one for you." As he said that he tossed it to me and I put it into the lever and turned it and then the barricade rose a centimeter but not enough to get above.

I went back to look and soon I had found it and I went to the lever and put the last key in and the barricade went over the lava keeping it from coming down.

We crossed the lava bed, and then it started melting through the metal. We went through the door on the opposite side. As we went down the hallway, we started seeing pictures on the walls.

However, there was one picture that stood out from the rest, it was a picture of a skeleton woman in a dress and at that moment I knew it had to be the dead man's daughter.

As I looked forward, I could see a light up ahead and as we went into the light, I noticed it was a clearing.

This clearing was in an enormous cavern and in the clearing there were a bunch of hills and trees as far as the eye could see.

There was one hill that stood out though and that is because it was glistening like it was raining on which was impossible because we were inside the earth.

I went up to the hill with the others following me and as soon as I got to it I got the urge to run to the top.

I began walking and before I knew it I was at the top of the hill and I knew what I had to do, I ran down the other side and before I knew it I was falling and I had landed in a heap and started laughing.

The others came to see if I was okay but saw that I was laughing and started laughing themselves.

I looked up and in front of me was a flower that was blooming...wait a second in the bloom was a chest.

I turned around and opened the chest and inside was a piece of paper that read: past the silver lake and the decision that you'll have to make, up a stair and down two and you'll find the third note too.

We started walking again, and after an hour we started thinking that we had made a wrong turn.

We took a left and then a right and saw that we had already been there so we turned around and took another left then a right and came into a room with jewels scattered on the ground.

We just went through that room and went into the next room and that room really caught my eye.

In the corner was a skeleton that sat on a throne and had a crown on his head. I went up to him and inspected him and I thought I knew him but I just couldn't put my finger on it.

As I walked away, it popped into my mind, the man on the throne was king George the second.

We went out the door on the right and started down that hallway and soon found the silver lake and I quickly figured out why they call it the silver lake.

It was called that because when the light hits it; the lake looks like liquid silver. We went past that and into the next hallway.

When we got into the next hallway, we started going farther into the earth because the rock walls turned from brown to bright red.

We continued walking until we came up to a fork in the road. Danyelle pointed at the one on the right, and Athero pointed to the one on the left.

I thought for a second and then went with the one on the left and soon we found ourselves face to face with a giant slope.

We slid down the slope and soon found ourselves up close to the first staircase. We tried walking up it but soon found out that it was a trick staircase.

I searched for a button, and after a few tries, I finally found it. When I hit it, the stairs turned back to normal, and I climbed up them to the second level.

I started walking again as soon as the others got up to where I was and then soon I could see the second staircase, but this one would go down.

We reached it an hour into the walk and when we got there; we started climbing, but like the other one, it was a trick stair but in reverse. When I tried to go onto it, it just flung me back onto the top stair. Then I started looking for the button that would make this stair regular.

After a long search for the button, I sat down and, to my relief, the stairs changed and I realized I had sat on the button making it switch.

I walked down the stairs and then after them I came across yet another set of stairs that also went down.

Fortunately, the third staircase button was already done, and I didn't have to do anything but walk down the stairs to my next task.

I looked around because the clue said that there was a note here, so I started searching and that is when I noticed the lever.

I pulled the lever and out of nowhere came a box that fell from the sky. I looked at it because it looked extremely old and it was of old wood.

I opened the box and as soon as I did dust flew everywhere and then I saw the note that read: past the hills and out the door, don't you dare slip on the floor, pass the crystals and the diamond wreath and go through and you will find the next clue?

We started walking again, and then something caught my eye, but I didn't go. Instead, I went to the door, and that is when I noticed it needed a lever to open it.

It was then that I realized that the thing that had caught my eye was part of the lever so I went back to where It had caught my eye and found that it didn't this time so I went over to it and sure enough there was a diamond laying on the ground.

I picked it up and then I saw a small pole sticking out of the ground and so I went over there next and saw that it was also part of the pole that would open the door and it had a screw on part and I thought it must be where the diamond goes.

I pulled the diamond out of my pocket and screwed it onto the pole and I saw it fit perfectly, but there was one more piece to find by the looks of it.

I started having a look around and soon I had found the last piece of the pole sticking out of a hole in the ground and I hooked it together with the other one.

Then I walked back to the door and put the pole into the hole in the door and turned the pole. When I did that, it opened, and I went through it into another hallway.

When we went into the hallway, we were almost blinded because the floor was so bright, as if someone still lived here.

We walked across the floor as quietly as we could and then Athero knocked over a plate and then we heard the low rumbling of rocks and a voice that said "who is there "

We didn't want to find out who was talking, so we went through the door in a hurry and found ourselves in a hallway that had rubies along the walls. So we went into the next room and found sapphires in this one.

Then we hit a fork in the road, so we went left and we found emeralds on the walls.

We kept going, but we didn't find any diamonds, just other gems like opal, Valspar, and garnet. So we were about to turn around when we got to this enormous room that had about a billion diamonds in it, but there was no wreath, so we just kept going.

We went through the hall and were about to give up when we walked into a second room filled with diamonds and on top was the diamond wreath that the note was talking about.

We walked up to the wall, and I started looking at the diamonds on the wall and I saw that there was a door inside of it. I touched the diamond, and the door started came forward.

When the door surfaced, the diamonds shifted and made way for it. I opened the door and inside was a box. I grabbed the box and went to open it, but before I could open it, an enormous wind appeared and disappeared just as fast.

I tried a couple more times, then I got a good look at the box and it had a satyr on it and so I told Danyelle to get the box and for once it didn't blow her away.

She opened it and inside was a gold tablet (for once it wasn't a paper)that she read with us over her shoulder: go past the waterfall and down the metal hall down the ladder that is made of gold but, don't be bold, up the hill and across the quicksand, use the boat and you'll get the third note.

We went into the next room and started looking for a door and soon we found it on the far wall. We went through it and found ourselves in yet another clearing.

We started having a look around in the clearing and soon found out that it had a waterfall. As we passed the waterfall, we noticed the door that was open, but as we got close to it, the door started closing.

Then I noticed the two buttons that were on both sides of the doors, so I stood on one as Athero stood on the other one and then as we stepped on the buttons, a secret door opened.

When the door opened, we went through it and found ourselves in a room with a table that was full of food. I started stepping forward and began going up the hill on the other side and as I did immediately; I started sinking, and I knew it was the quicksand that was mentioned in the note.

We started moving and then I remembered what they say about quicksand, the more you move the faster you sink so I grabbed a vine and started pulling myself up and after a few good minutes of good pulling I finally got out of the sand and back onto the hillside.

I scraped all the sand off my body and then continued towards the lake with the boat on the surface. In; the middle of the lake was an island and as we walked up to it, we started pulling the boat across the water and then the boat started pulling the other way, but there was no one pulling it.

We started pulling harder and the harder we pulled, the closer it came and as we did, we began seeing what was pulling in the opposite direction. Pulling on the other side was a dead body brought back to life.

We started pulling harder, and the boat came inland faster, and then we noticed the fog that was starting accumulating on the water around the boat.

We pulled as hard as we could and finally pulled the boat to the shore, where the dead body finally slid back to the depths of the lake.

We got into the boat and after a few minutes we started moving and pretty soon fog surrounded us and we couldn't see anywhere around us at all.

We couldn't even see if we were getting closer to the island. Then, suddenly, the fog began clearing to reveal a horrifying sight.

There were about a hundred dead bodies bobbing in the water, and as we got a closer look at them, we saw they were swimming in the water, just waiting for us.

As we got nearer to them, they started swimming towards the boat and started pulling on it, almost as if they were trying to make it sink.

When we finally reached the island, we it was full of treasure and boxes and I knew that the one that we needed was a silver or gold one.

We looked for a few moments and then found a gold one, but it was empty and so we kept on looking. Then we found a silver one, but it was also empty.

After; a few more chests of silver and gold, we finally found one that had something in it, but it was just a plank of wood and I tossed it without thinking.

Luckily, Danyelle caught it and started looking at it because she said, "Zack this is it...this is what we had to find...this is the next clue to the next note."

I took it from her and started looking it over and I saw she was right and I started reading: past the doors that have the puzzle, don't stop, the floor is going out you'll have to hustle, past the waterfall that is laden with gold and the trees that are covered in mold and you'll find the next note.

We started going forward through the door to the left and it opened up to a field that was smaller than that of the others that we had passed through before.

We started walking and soon we found the first part of the clue, the door with the puzzle and we started looking it over and soon we knew what we had to do.

We started looking for the pieces of a staff that would have to be metal or a really hard wood.

Then I looked around and saw a long stick that was also very thick sticking out of the ground. I tried to pull it out myself but it wouldn't budge and so I asked for help from the others.

Together, we pulled it out of the ground and we put it into the door and pushed left. When we did that, it moved to the left, and the lock began clicking and I knew we had the right limb.

We kept on pushing until the door began swinging open, revealing a hallway that had a door at the far end that looked like we could just push open.

We started walking down the hall, and the floor started giving out. With us walking on it and then I remembered the next part and it had said that we had to hustle.

We ran to the door at the far end of the hallway and opened it as the floor gave out right behind us. We were so relieved that we went through the door and found that we were in another part of the same field.

We walked a few moments, then I noticed the waterfall that had gold streaks in it and I walked past that and started for the woods, but as I got closer, I noticed that none of them had moss growing on them.

I turned around and was almost back to the others when I noticed that there were some trees on the edge of the wall of the cavern. I walked up to the trees and saw that the moss wasn't pointing north, so I went where the moss was pointing.

I went west because that is the way it was pointing. After; a few miles of walking, I finally reached some caves, and I went into each and everyone of them and soon I found a silver chest a few feet ahead of me.

I walked up to it and waited until the others were with me before I started reading and the others read over my shoulder as I read it in my head: this is the final note for this piece, in order to find the clue you'll have to go through the cave where purple meets red and the fire so hot that you can't even jump over them.

go down this hallway with all the doors and this clue you'll have found and you'll win another round, but first you'll have to find the two red keys that will open the door for the pole and it will have to go into the hands of Zeus.

We started walking and went through the door to the left in the cave wall and soon started seeing crystals.

First the crystals were rubies, then they slowly changed to sapphires, and then they changed again to emeralds and yet again to Valspar and then finally to amethyst, but there weren't any rubies meeting amethyst.

Then I saw a glint out of the corner of my eye and when I looked I saw the most beautiful thing. The two crystals merged into a more brilliant color.

I went to touch it but Danyelle had to pull me back as usual and then I snapped out of the trance and we started walking down the path and found ourselves on the edge of a cliff.

We edged ourselves across the cliff and soon we were on a wider ledge and we turned around and saw that in front of us were enormous cracks of hot lava vents.

I threw a rock across the vent and the rock evaporated on sight and I knew we had to cool it down.

I started looking around carefully not to go over any vents and after a while I got tired and hot from the vents being there and soon I saw a big water barrel but there was no way to get to it I could see.

I started going forward away from the vents and tripped on a string. Then the string broke and the water barrel spilled water all over the place, making the heat go away.

I went through the door on the other side and came into a hall that didn't have any doors at all, so we just kept going.

A few moments later we turned the corner and came to a door that was made of brass and had a silvery handle and as we opened the door, it squeaked a loud, high-pitched wail.

We went through the door and found ourselves in a hallway that had a lever base at the far end and I knew that this was where we had to find the keys.

I started opening up doors and soon found that it was a horrible idea, so we started forward and we went up to the base and looked it over and saw where we had to put the keys.

I started feeling the walls and soon I had found a secret room and on a pedestal in the corner was a gold laden box so I opened it.

Inside was the first red key. So I went back into the hallway and put the first red key into the base of the lever and then I turned it and one set of doors opened to the pole part of the lever.

I started looking for the second one and after a few minutes of searching; I found another secret room and in the center of the room was the silver chest that was laden with gold.

I went up to it and opened it and inside was the second key so I went back to the lever and put the second key into the lever and then turned the key and the second door opened revealing the pole part for the lever and I put it in place (with a little help from the others of course) and pulled and for a few minutes it was too heavy for me to lift and then as I gathered my strength I finally got it opened and I saw a tablet in the base.

I reached into it and pulled the tablet out of the chest and I read: past the diner's table and the hunter's best, go up to the dead man and reach inside his vest. Inside, you'll find a marble or two and this will make you get through.

We went through a door that had opened the moment that the lever was down and we started walking down another hallway and soon we came upon this room that was overflowing with coins of all sorts and there was gold all over the place and in the center was a table big enough to fit a hundred men and it looked like it was of mahogany with cedar legs.

Although the table was nice looking, that wasn't what caught my eye. The table was now covered with bountiful food.

We went to the door to the right and soon we were in a room that had animals strung up by their feet upside down and we just ran through that room with our hands over our noses in that part of the clue.

When we got to the other side, we went through the door and found ourselves in a skeleton chamber, and the first thing I saw were the skeletons littering the room and after a few more minutes of searching for the one with a vest on we finally found the one that we were looking for. I went over to him and soon found everything I could except for what I was supposed to find.

I searched him one more time and found out that he had a hidden pocket and I tried to find it and then I unzipped his vest and found that his vest had a pocket on the inside.

I undid his pocket and reached inside and inside were two clear marbles that were pretty big.

I walked past the other skeletons and soon I was in a room that had a couple of Hera statues and one each of them one eye was gone.

I gave one eye to Athero, and we started trying to climb the statues so we could put the eyes back in.

Once I got to the head of the statue, I climbed around to the front and Athero did the same thing.

As we put the eyes in their sockets, a light went between their beams and shot a beam down towards the wall and as it did, a door slid to the side and we slowly got down in case the ground was a trap.

We walked across, watching our step, and went through that door. When we went through that door, it slammed behind us and we walked further in and soon we saw the next piece of the shield of Zeus lay untouched.

I began walking up there to it but axes swinging soon stopped me as they were swinging back and forth... back and forth. I started thinking and then, out of nowhere, I started counting.

As soon as I got to five, I made a jump and landed right in between the axes. I did this repeatedly until I had reached the shield piece.

As I got onto the first step, the axes stopped and the others could come where I was. As soon as we were there, I grabbed the shield piece and put it into my bag and I heard a clink and a zap and then as soon as I heard that, I looked into my bag and I saw that the shield pieces were "one".

I had Athero pull out the map and as soon as he did the marking that said, The Temple of Zeus was check marked and a new one appeared that read statue of Zeus.

I looked at the others and nodded, and then dug out a transport marble and threw it into the air. When we did, it made a portal to Athens like I wanted and we went through right into the rain.

CHAPTER 5

STATUE OF ZEUS

We quickly got out of the rain and waited for it to stop. When it did, we went to the local pub and asked them where the statue of Zeus was.

They didn't seem to notice, but they pointed towards the corner of the pub and we looked and saw that they were pointing to a large building with a single statue that was falling apart.

We walked up to the building and the first thing that I noticed and that I pointed out was the sign that seemed to cover up something glowing.

` I walked up to it and pulled the sign off and quickly motioned for the others to come to me and then I touched the glyph and pulled into the darkness. When I landed, it was in the water, so I started treading water and looking for land.

The only fact was there wasn't any shore, so I looked under the water and I saw that there was a tunnel that led down.

I began hearing screaming, and I looked up and saw the others falling and they were going to land on top of me if I didn't move. So I did.

When they landed and they surfaced, I told them we had to take the tunnel that was under us.

I dove, and the others followed and together we went deeper into the water and then we surfaced like we were going back up, but when we surfaced, it was a totally different scene.

For one, the room wasn't dark, and it was lush with green and crystals and on the wall was the note for the first clue.

I read it as clear as day in my head: out of the water and down the hall across the field and to the waterfall and you shall find the note to the first clue.

We waded out of the water and started out onto the grass, and then I noticed that there were two halls.

We started down one hall and then we started seeing pictures of bad things, so we got together and started talking and finally I made a decision that we needed to go down the other hallway instead.

When we went down this hall, we saw a light up ahead and soon we came out into a field, but this one didn't have a waterfall, so we just continued on our journey.

We went through the doors at the far end of the field and soon we were in another field and as the last one, this one also didn't have a waterfall.

We walked through yet another door and then Danyelle noticed we had already passed this area and that we were going in circles.

That is when I noticed the other door to the right and I went through it and pulled the others towards it when I did.

We went through it and found ourselves in a third field that had three waterfalls, each one larger than the rest. We went to the closest one first and went to go into it, but found that behind the first waterfall was a wall.

By the time that I had figured out that there was a wall there, I was soaking wet.

I went to the next one and there was a cave behind it, but it was almost empty except for a few things that were by the walls and then we left that cave and went out of the waterfall, getting soaked again by it.

We walked to the biggest one of them all and went to go through it but it also had a wall, so we went back to the last waterfall we did and started looking around again and soon found a lever that opened up a secret room.

We went into the secret room and after a few minutes of looking we found a lever that made a pedestal raise from the found and on the pedestal was a button that uncovered a puzzle and after a minute or two we figured out that we needed two keys.

We went to look through the boxes and crates and then I found the first key in the corner under a barrel like crate and then I went to the pedestal and put the first key into it.

When I did, the pedestal sank about halfway into the ground and then stopped. Then I went looking for the second key and soon I heard Danyelle running toward me and as she got close to me, she slipped and fell with the key in hand.

she got up and stabilized herself and then gave me the second key as she fell again and then as she got up she said "I'm going to wait outside".

Then she left, and I went to the pedestal and put the key into place and the pedestal started sinking below the surface of the cave floor and then a panel came across the hole and the note was on it.

I picked it up and looked at it in the light and read: down through the door at the end of the field, pass the skeletons through that door and you'll need a key and there on the ground, the clue will be.

We began looking or a doorway of some sort and after a few hours of looking I looked at some vines that were covering up some of the wall and when I did I discovered a little hole that was only

big enough for one at a time.

I pulled the others to where I thought the hole was, but I had lost it and I told them to "keep close" and I started searching for it again. After a few more moments, I found the hole again, and I motioned for the others to come to me and then I went into the hole and went through to the other side.

When I got to the other side, I waited for the others to get through and as they emerged; I pulled them out, and we started walking again.

Then we found our way back to the first field that we were in before the one with the waterfalls and I saw the door that we had to go through and walked across the field but as we got down to the door, it disappeared in a wisp of smoke and then appeared a few feet away from us.

We went through the door. A few minutes of walking later, we came into a room that was full of jewels, but there wasn't any door except for the one that we had come out of and that was behind us.

We started searching for the way out of that room, but all we could find were boxes and vases and jewels that were in piles across the room.

Then suddenly, a door opened, and I looked around. When I looked around, I saw Athero had lifted a vase and apparently it had a button under it.

We went through that door and it led to a hallway and it seemed to go on forever and when we finally made it to the end of the hallway; we noticed it was a rock wall with a glyph on it so we touched it and it brought us to yet another room without an exit.

We searched for the exit and I picked up anything that I could find and soon I found the crate that was hiding the switch. I pulled the switch but nothing happened and then I noticed the keyholes and I knew we had to find a couple of keys to put one on both sides. I started looking for the first key and I had thought that I had looked everywhere when I heard feet rushing towards me so I turned around and saw Athero walking towards me rather fast.

He walked up to me and handed me the key that went into the first keyhole and turned it and it also went down halfway. Then we went back to searching, this time for the second key. I began throwing things every which way and after a few good hours of looking; we were about to give up when I just sat down on what I thought was a crate. Turns out it was a treasure chest that was half covered with treasure and there was only a little piece peeking out.

I cleared it of treasure and inspected the chest and I noticed it was an odd shape and it needed a weird key of some sort so I went and continued on to look for that key and I found it almost immediately put into a box that said "do not open". We took the key and when we did, we almost opened the box that said that.

We slammed it shut just in time to see a monster trying to get out. When we put the key into the chest and turned it; we opened the chest and inside was the second key to the pedestal. I went back down to the pedestal and put the last key into the keyhole and turned it. Then the pedestal sank into the ground and then a gold plank came across and on the plank was a key and I knew we would need this somewhere down the road so I stuck it in my pocket and as I did a door opened to the right of me.

    I motioned for the others to follow, and soon we were in another hallway. Half an hour later, walking down this hall, we came walking by some skeletons that had darts in them and I felt my foot go down and so I looked at my feet and that is when I heard them release.

    We all started running and then I saw a door up ahead, but as we got closer, we saw it needed a key. Then I remembered I had a key.

    I put the key into the lock and to my amazement it turned and opened and we went through and that is when we found out that we were in a temple of some sort. There In the middle of the room was a pedestal and there was a tablet on it and as we walked up to it, the darn thing began shining.

    When the glare cleared off of the tablet, I picked it up and read to the others: go down the hall that is to the left and through a tunnel and you'll end up at a chasm, cross the chasm and solve the puzzle and you'll get the note to the second clue.

We started looking in the direction that it had implied and soon found a hidden door. As soon as we got it open, we left the clearing that we were in.

We turned a corner and soon we were going down a dark hallway and we had to go as slow as we could bent over because the ceiling of the hall was a short one (the only reason we knew that is because Danyelle banged her head on it.)

We crept down the hall and after a few minutes of bending over; the ceiling went higher and we could straighten up again.

After a few minutes of pure darkness, we began seeing a speck of light in the dark and then we emerged

Onto a cliff and on the other side I could see the lever that would open the door for the second note.

I looked around again and saw a ledge that we could scoot across, so maybe we could get to where we could cross the chasm.

We began scooting across the ledge, and when we finally made it across, we were heartbroken to find that it wasn't there.

So we went back the way we came and as I looked back, I saw a door had opened to another part of the ledge.

I nudged Danyelle, and she showed everyone that there was a new way to get across and we started back to the door that had just opened and soon we were in another hallway that was dimly lit and I could see the end, but barely.

As we exited the hallway, I saw we were in yet another room that also had a ledge, so I pointed at the ledge and told them, "come on".

We edged across the ledge and found ourselves a little closer to the other side of the chasm.

when we reached the other end of the ledge was another hallway but this one was a little different as an old man guarded it and I knelt down and asked the man his name and when I did he changed form.

When he changed form, he was a fire monster, and he was blocking the entrance to the tunnel.

We had to block him and then I asked Athero, "what do we do now"

He just shrugged and dodged another blow and I said, "you don't know, but you are a son of Athena."

Then, in between blocks, he took off a medal that he had on his neck and tossed it to me.

When I read it back and it said Ceares then suddenly it was gone and so was the monster.

All that it left was the fires that it was making, but there was still a problem; there was a red furious fire blocking the entrance.

I looked at Athero and then at Danyelle and then Athero walked right through the fire as if there was nothing there.

I went to go through the fire but I hesitated and I got burned. Then I looked at them and they said, "don't hesitate and you will walk right through as well."

I tried again, but this time I didn't hesitate and I found myself on the other side next to my friends and we began walking again.

As we walked, I started seeing light and when we came into the light; I saw we were on the other side of the chasm, and I knew we were getting close to finding the note.

We looked all over and saw that there was a pile of boxes in a corner, so we went through them and soon we found an old chest that was also made of wood.

I opened it and saw that there was a scroll inside and I passed it to Danyelle and she read, "go past this box and through the wall, down the hall past the crystals and through the waterfall and you'll find the second clue."

We all glanced at the wall at the same time and after a few minutes I just walked up to the wall and took a deep breath and walked right through.

I waited for the others to follow and then I tried to go back but it wouldn't let me so I just hollered through and said "you just have to trust me and trust yourself."

Almost as soon that I felt a powerful gust of air and then Danyelle appeared in front of me with Athero not far behind.

As soon as they were with me again, we started walking with as little as we could see and as soon as our lighting got better; we stopped hanging onto walls and started for where the light was coming from.

We continued walking and then suddenly we were in a lit up cave and I saw the lights were coming from the crystals that were there.

We started looking at the crystals and soon we were stuck looking at the crystals and I was the first one to snap out of it and soon I saw everyone was looking at the crystals.

I pulled everyone away from the crystals one by one and pulled them into the next room and as soon as I did that, they all came back to reality and I had to tell them what happened; the crystals had hypnotized them.

Then we started walking again and soon we came across the biggest crystal that I've ever seen.

I walked up to it and started feeling it and soon was hooked and couldn't move away and they had to pull me away and sit me down and after a few minutes I came back to reality again and I knew what had happened and again we started walking.

A few moments later, we were walking silently down another hall and it seemed to last forever and when we finally got out of the hall; we came into a clearing but there was not a single waterfall in sight.

At the other side of the clearing was a door, but it had a metal gate around it and then I saw the lever that we had to pull but it was missing a piece and we probably had to find it.

We started searching for the missing piece and soon Danyelle had found it and we went over to the lever and I had her put the missing piece in and I pulled the lever.

But it still wouldn't budge and then, as I was walking away, I heard a clicking sound .

I turned around and Danyelle was pulling the lever and I thought to myself, "I could have known the person who found the missing piece is the only person who can pull it."

With the switch pulled down, she turned to me and smiled and I turned to the gate and saw that it was now open.

We went through the gate and into another piece of the field and I didn't see any waterfall on this one either.

Then I noticed that there were traps on the ground and soon as I noticed the traps started going off and one almost went off on my foot.

Then I noticed the button on the far wall and I knew what I had to do; I had to push it and all the traps would stop going off.

I raced toward the button as fast as I could and as soon as I reached it; I noticed that there were two traps right in front of it.

So I spread my legs and pushed the button as hard as I could and then I saw all the traps stop immediately and the others walked up to me.

Then I noticed a door had opened in front of us and we went through it to find another part of the field and this one had a waterfall in it.

We went through the field to the waterfall and as soon as we were upon it, the waterfall split in two and we could walk through without getting wet.

We saw that there was a cave behind the waterfall and in the cave there was a chest that I saw was holding a shining tablet, just like the last clue.

We walked up to it and opened the chest, and the light inside of it was blinding. So we had to cover our eyes for a few minutes until the light had shuttered down.

When it had dimmed down far enough that I could read it I picked it up and read" across the field you shall find a door, down the hall and across the floor and past the gold, silver and past the three eyed goat and you shall find the third note."

We went across the field and soon we found the door that it had mentioned and went through it and found ourselves in a hallway.

The hallway seemed to last forever, like most of the halls we have been through, and soon we were on our way to the next part of the clue.

When we came out into the open, amazed at the artwork on the walls and we looked around and found that these could be at least a thousand years old.

We started crossing the walkway but suddenly stopped by a chimera and I rushed in, uncapping my marker and turned it into a sword and I went for its heart but the beast hit me with its tail and I went flying across the room.

When I landed, I still had my sword in hand and I went after it again, but this time I had the upper hand because it was facing the others and I first cut off its snake tail, then each of its heads.

` When I did that, it dropped dead, and we continued our quest and soon we were in a room with a bunch of gold, but there was no other way out.

So we started looking for the way out or something that would make the way out.

I looked everywhere and soon I started looking at the piles of gold and found a box that had a key inside it and then I saw the wall that had a keyhole in it.

I walked down the pile and put the key into the keyhole and it started widening as soon as I turned it and it turned into a doorway and Danyelle said "good job".

We went through the door into another hallway and this one didn't have any light at all and then we hit a rock wall and I pushed and it moved.

As I was pushing, it moved outward until it was out of the way and we moved into the next room. This room was unique because it's filled with silver.

I reached up to the biggest silver pile, and I found another box, but this one was holding a button and I pushed it and the button started glowing and so I figured it was a hide and seek thing.

I went one way, and the light went dimmer, and then I went another and it got brighter and then started getting dimmer again.

So I started turning until it was lit again and I started walking that way and the farther I went, the brighter it got and then I saw I was in a hallway and I could hear the others hollering for me.

I hollered back and said go to the sound of my voice and soon I felt a big blast of wind and I barely got out of the way as the others came running through.

As soon as they were in the same hall as I was we started looking for the way into the next room and we continued walking looking as we went and soon I fell into a door and soon I had the others on top of me like a domino effect.

When everyone was up and walking again, we noticed we were in the last room and I saw the goat in the corner and it seemed to watch us.

We went up to it and then Danyelle pointed and said, "look it's on a lever" and we moved the goat and went back to the lever and pulled it and a door opened and it had a note inside the hallway opening.

We walked up to it and then I picked it up and read to the others: down this hall and past the rubies at the end of the wall and down a great waterfall where you shall send and you will find the third clue at the end.

We started walking and soon we were at the end of the hall and soon we ended at the end of the hall and landed in a room that had gems all over the place, but there was one gem missing, the ruby.

We continued walking again because the last time we stopped to admire the gems; we got fixed on them and we were not taking that chance again.

We walked towards the wall and it opened and we went into another hallway, which this time wasn't very long.

A few minutes later we were in a smaller room, but this one stored rubies on the far wall and I knew we had to pass them.

We went past them with no trouble and then we ran into a waterfall but it wasn't as big as it said so we walked right past and started up a big slope and on the top we saw the waterfall that it talked about but it looked really far away.

We started walking and soon we came to a second waterfall that was a bigger one and we tried to cross it, but it started sweeping us away.

We barely got out of the water on the other side before it had swept us out into the tide.

We started walking again in our wet clothes and then we saw a small river ahead and we just walked across because it was too small to sweep us away, unlike the last one.

When we landed on the other side, we could see the waterfall that we were supposed to go down in the distance, but we still had a way to go.

We began walking again and came across this weird creature and she smiled and disappeared and then we came to the roaring waterfall and we started having a look at the waterfall. Then Danyelle said; I have to go down that?"

I nodded and then we started looking for a way to go down the waterfall without getting hurt.

A minute passed, and we found something. We took one look at the board that we had found and went back to looking.

We came back another minute later and looked at the waterfall and again went back to look and then I went back to the waterfall and saw a barrel near the edge, but there was only room for one person.

I set the barrel aside and started helping look for one for Danyelle and we quickly emerged with another barrel and then we found one more for Athero and we all jumped into our barrels and started drifting down the river and almost forgot to put our lids on.

We drifted down the river and then after about ten minutes of going; I started wondering if we were going anywhere, so I unscrewed my lid and saw that I'd gotten caught on a branch.

I was also a few feet from the edge, so If I unhooked myself from the branch manually, then I would go off the waterfall with my lid unscrewed.

I screwed my lid on again and began rocking in my barrel and soon I was free and then I felt myself go off the edge and into a deep pool.

I unscrewed my lid and saw that I had bobbed under the waterfall and had come out on the other side.

When I saw I was on the other side, I got out of my barrel and climbed onto the cave inside and started exploring because there were tons of stuff inside other than boxes and a chest.

I went immediately to the chest but had to call the others to it as well but once I had done that I opened the chest and I passed the glowing clue to Athero and he read to us: after you read this go through the door on the left and go forth and hold your breath because there will be gas, go through to the door to the right and you'll find the mask and then up a hill and down two and you will find the note to the fourth clue.

We started looking around and soon found the door that it was talking about and it opened a little, so we waited for it to open and this foul odor started coming from the door and I knew it was the gas.

We started holding our breath and soon we came to the next room and I saw the door to the room with the masks immediately and I darted for it because I couldn't hold my breath much longer.

Danyelle and Athero followed me into the next room and closed the door behind us, and then we saw the masks and we went to them at once.

We put them on and as soon as we put them on, we let out a breath of relief and went back to the first room and with our masks on we could search for the next part.

We went around and then I noticed the print on the wall that there was a lever that was magically broken in three pieces and three keys to pull it.

We started looking for the first part and soon found it on top of a pile of junk and I started looking for somewhere to put it and after a few minutes I found a hole in the ground in the center of the room and I put the first part of the lever in the hole.

Then we started looking for the second part of the lever and after about an hour, I heard Athero rushing to me and he had the second piece in hand and he gave it to me.

I went to connect it to the last one and sure enough, it connected, and it became one with the first one. We went back to looking, but this time we were looking for the third part of the lever and any of the keys.

Right off the bat, Danyelle went up to me and I saw she had the third piece in her hand. So I took it from her and went to connect it and like the first one, it went right together and made the lever and it started forming the keyholes.

We started looking for the keys now and I knew from the keyholes that there were four, not three, like we thought to be found.

THE SHIELD OF ZEUS

We continued looking for about thirty minutes and then were about to give up when I sat down and something pricked me.

I got up and saw something partly sticking out of the ground, so I pulled at it and soon I had it part of the way out of the ground and I saw it was a hand holding onto a key.

I knew it had to be one key that went to the lever, so I pried it off the hand.

I put it into the keyhole and started searching for the second key and Danyelle found it behind some walls and she brought it to me and I put it in the lever and then started searching for the third one and after a few minutes Danyelle found the third one and I said to her "girl you are on fire today".

Then I took that one, but it didn't fit in the third keyhole, so I tried to put it into the fourth keyhole and it fit snugly and I knew I had to find the third key because we had found all the others.

We started search and soon found the last one and I put it in the last keyhole and turned them one by one and then we all took a hold of the shaft and pulled but it didn't need all of us because it basically pulled itself.

When we got the lever down, a door opened, and we found a hilly courtyard and we started going through the courtyard and soon we saw the hill that we had to climb and it was a big one too.

We started climbing and an hour later we were at the top and we started going down,and when we got to the bottom; we had a little surprise because the bottom was actually the middle and we had to go down another hill.

When we noticed this we sighed and started going down the second hill and as soon as we were at the final bottom we were facing a box and I looked around to make sure that the others were listening.

I opened the box and inside was a note that read: down the ladder and through the hall, down the stairs and past the saws, into the room that is full of delusion but make no mistake and make no confusion and you find the fourth clue.

We started walking again and after a few minutes of walking; we stumbled upon an old ladder, but it looked like it was going to break at any moment.

I started looking around and soon stumbled onto some rope and I brought it back to the ladder and went to put it down the hole and found the others already at the bottom.

When I asked how they got down, they just said use the ladder it's more sturdy than it looks so I put my first foot on it and thought "something doesn't feel right".

I looked out of the corner of my eye and saw my friends tied up behind a tree and then I looked down again and the others at the bottom had disappeared, replaced by monsters and I took my feet out of the hole in time to see it slam shut.

I looked up to see a monster standing over me and I got back in time to feel the wind coming off of its claws.

It kept on swinging and I just dodged every one swing and then I went to the others and saw they were bound with a slip knot.

I pulled the knot out and then one by one we went down the hole and landed in a pool of water.

We started swimming for shore and as soon as we got there; we noticed that the water didn't make our clothes wet.

We crawled out of the water and saw a door leading off to another room, and so we went to the hall that it led to.

We went down the hallway that came out of the cave that the pond was in and we came out in a really dangerous room and it had saws everywhere.

We started walking and soon we were about sawed in half but Danyelle pulled me out of the way and then I returned the favor a few minutes later.

By making her duck below some. Once we almost got sawed a few more times, and I had to save the others a few more times, we finally got out of that room and into another hallway.

We started going forward and soon we found ourselves at a staircase and so we went down and after a few moments of walking down, we leveled out again and saw that we were in a doorway that led to a room that bent the laws of reality.

Once we had entered the room, we saw that there were stairs going every which way and we had to find which was the right one.

I looked it over and saw the door that we had to go through to get the clue, but I didn't see the way to get there.

I continued to look, but I still didn't have any luck at all, so I took a set of stairs to see where it got me and to my delight it got me on the right set of stairs but the wrong side.

So I went back through the door but ended up somewhere other than where I was before. So I tried a couple more times and then I finally arrived on the right set of stairs and on the right side of the set of stairs.

I went through the door on that set of stairs and wound up in a room that had a single crate inside of it and it was not open, so I found a chisel and a rock and started prying it open.

When I finally got it open, the others had joined me inside the room and they helped me pull the chest out of the crate and onto the ground.

When we got it onto the ground I opened it and read: past the statues that will meet you on the eye and go past the first set of stairs and down the second then up the third and past the flying birds, go walking and do what you do and you'll find the note to the fifth clue.

We started walking again and soon we were in a long hallway that we had to feel our way down. So, after a few minutes of feeling our way down, Danyelle found a torch on the wall and she handed it to me to light it. When I lit it, the first thing I noticed was the enormous statues, and they seem to look at us.

Then their eyes began sparking and as we moved on, they seemed to follow us and I remembered the first part of the note and kept on walking with my chin held high.

Then, as we were going away from the statues, their eyes began fading away.

As we started walking again, we came to a triple hallway but two of the hallways didn't have stairs on them so we took the one that did but it didn't seem to be that simple so we backtracked and went through the one that didn't have stairs.

A few minutes of walking later, we came upon a staircase going up and there was an arrow that was pointed up and then the others started going up the stairs.

I quickly pointed them in the right direction and after a few minutes of walking we came to another staircase but this one went down and I told the others, "this one you can go down" and I led the way.

As we descended the stairs, we began seeing that the walls were changing again from dark red to brown, and then we found ourselves in a hallway that was a little different from that of the others.

In; the center of the room was a beautiful grand stair that is made of crystal and the note said that we had to go up this one as well, so we did and found a door at the top that was partly open.

I opened it the rest of the way and found myself in an underground forest and I could hear the birds chirping from far away.

We started walking and soon I started seeing shapes in the trees and then I looked up and I could make out the shape of a bird flying just overhead.

Then I noticed the light coming from a tree trunk and so I went up to it and stuck my hand inside and pulled out a little box and I gave it to Danyelle to open because satyrs are much better at deflecting magic than humans.

She opened it and we gathered around her and read: go through due south and into the clearing and you shall find the lever that will open the door to the fifth clue.

When we had finished reading she put the box down and we started walking again and it didn't take long at all to find south and we followed south for a couple of hours and what seemed like an eternity, we finally reached the edge of the forest and found a wall that wasn't mentioned in the note.

We went along the wall and soon found a hallway so we went into the hall because we had no choice as we were in a hot spot and we had no other way to go.

When we got into the tunnel, we soon found a hallway, out that we were in an underground tunnel and we started looking for a way up.

A few minutes I found it with a little of Danielle's help and we all climbed out of the tunnel and into the clearing and I could see the door that held the next clue.

We started making our way towards it and then we saw it was like the last one and we needed to find the lever pieces and piece them together and pull it.

It didn't take us long, and we had all the pieces and we put them into the hole and pulled. When we did, the door opened, and we walked inside and started having a look around.

Soon we had found the tablet that was on the pedestal this time and it was as shiny as ever and she read: past the doors and down the hall across the fountain and follow the call and you shall find the note to the sixth clue.

We started going to the door, but then we started noticing that there were many doors and each one had a symbol above it and after a few moments of thinking, I figured it out.

Above each door had a symbol of a god it represented, and the god we were trying to find the weapon of was Zeus, so all we had to do was go through the door with the Zeus symbol above it.

We found the one with a lightning bolt above the door and we went through it and then we started walking again and soon we came across the same thing except with hallways so we looked over the symbols and found the lightning bolt and started down that hallway.

When we were about halfway down the hall, we could hear water running, but we still couldn't see it.

We turned a corner, and soon we saw we were coming upon a brick wall.

As we got up to it I touched it but nothing happened so, I stepped back and a stone went down and that usually means something bad.

Instead, the wall began opening, revealing a fountain that was huge and we had to walk to the other side of it.

We began walking and as soon as we did we started getting wet and as we were walking there were brief pauses where the water would stop and then it would burst out soaking us. A few hours later of constant soaking, we finally made it to the end, and we heard a low bird and I knew it was the call and so I started following the sound.

I soon came to a hole in the ground and I put my head down the hole and before I knew it, I was falling right into a pool.

I started swimming towards where the sound was coming from and it was coming from under me and I dove under the water and saw that the water had naiads in it and at the bottom was the chest.

I yelled for the others to come on down and soon I heard the others splash down and I dove to get the box at the bottom of the pond but it seemed to have magic in it so I surfaced and asked Danyelle to do it and we swam to the shore.

Right after we had got to shore I went back into the water to help Danyelle carry the chest and together we put it on the shore and she opened it and read: go past the crystals in the caves and the diamonds in the mines and you shall go into the clearing and pull the lever and you shall find the sixth clue.

Once we read it, the note turned into ashes and blew away, and we started walking again.

A few minutes passed, and we came across a cave that was full of crystals such as rubies and emeralds. We knew we had found the crystal cave, and we had to move past it.

We pushed on and for a while we didn't see a thing else that would relate to that factor and when we were about to double back; we came to another cave with crystals, but this one had sapphires and garnet in it .

We started walking right past that one and in the distance I could see a light that kept flickering, but we seemed to walk slowly towards it.

When we finally got there, I saw that the blinking lights were actually diamonds in the piles of rubble on the side of the hallway and I knew it had to be the diamond mines and they must have collapsed because of diametric pressure.

We walked past it into the clearing ahead and I saw the door up ahead and I went up to it and that is when I saw the hole that the lever would go in.

When the others caught up to me, I pointed at the hole and said," well we might start looking."

We started looking and soon we had found the first out of two it was looking like and we put it into the hole but it didn't fit and that is when I noticed it had a screw on a piece that we still had to find.

We started looking again and soon I heard Athero say, "geez look how big this diamond is."

I took it from him and saw that there was an indention in it and I put it onto the lever and screwed it on and then put it into the hole.

This time it stayed, and we pushed it and the door opened to reveal another little room that wasn't as big as the last one.

We began looking for the tablet and soon found it in a chest that was in a corner. We went up to it and I opened it and pulled out the tablet and waited for the shine to go away and then I read: go past the lake and through the waterfall and under the bridge you'll find a door that hides the note for the seventh clue.

We looked around but didn't see any lake in sight. Then we turned around a cave and saw it just sitting there and we walked up to it and we started thinking about what the second part of the tablet said: the waterfall.

We started walking but there wasn't any waterfall in sight so we just kept on walking and as soon as we turned around we saw it, the most amazing (moving) waterfall and we went to go through it and then I noticed it would kill us to go through it because it wasn't water it was acid.

I pulled Danyelle back right as she was about to jump through it and then she noticed it as well and thanked me for it.

We started looking again and soon we came across a waterfall that was pouring from a cliff and I went through it followed by the others and on the other side we found a sacred place that had a little creek going through and a bridge going over it.

We went over to the bridge and we went under it to investigate and sure enough there was a door and it was unlocked so we opened the door and pulled out a chest and inside was a single note that read: go past the locked door and through the cave of red and blue and past what is old and knew and through the door of golden lore and you will find the seventh clue.

We started walking again and soon we found a door that was shut and we soon found out that it was the locked door that was in the note to the clue.

We started walking again, and I went ahead of the others and found a hole in the side wall and so I went through and found myself in a cave.

I went forward into the cave and in the far end I could see glittering and so I went farther in and saw that the glittering was rubies and sapphires but I knew better than to dwindle so I went past it and found myself in a big room.

We started looking around the room and almost as soon as we came into the room and started looking around; I noticed that there were skeletons in cages and then I saw the lever.

I went up to the lever and tried to pull it, but it wouldn't budge, so I asked the others for help and soon we had the lever pulled down to its maximum length.

Once we had the lever down the wall in front of us rippled and I stuck my hand out to touch it and when I did, it pulled me through.

When I reached the other side of the wall, I saw I was in another room and this one had like a mirror and I noticed it had letters beside it on the wall.

I thought to myself that it had to be the door of golden lore. I read the golden words out loud to the others: through this door you will find the seventh clue.

When I read those words, I saw the mirror ripple and then made a doorway and when I saw it; I went through and found myself in another room that was a lot smaller than the last.

In the corner was a chest, so I waited for the others to come through and then together we went to the chest and I opened it and it held yet another shining tablet.

I waited for the shining tablet to calm down and then I read: down this road and through a wall down the stairs that leads to the great hall, fall through a hole that you cannot miss and you will have the last note at your fingertips.

We looked around but didn't see any hall and then I saw a wall coming down and we started walking towards it. Then I heard a blast of air and I knew that something was being released.

I looked around and saw that it was arrows and I knew what I had to do and I ran with the others on my heels. Thankfully, we all got across safely.

When we were all safe in the hall, we went to walk down it and soon we were near the end and I couldn't see a thing and then I started seeing a blinking light.

As we got closer, I noticed that the blinking light was a wall with a glyph on it and I knew somehow that it was the wall that we had to go through so I reached out and touched it and immediately I found myself in a different room.

As soon as I went through, I noticed I was on top of a staircase and I started going down them with my friends behind me and then suddenly the stairs turned into a slide and we began sliding down right into a hole.

When we landed, I noticed we were in a pond beneath the room that we were in and we started swimming for shore.

When we got to shore we started toward the light at the far end of the room and I knew that there had to be something in that room.

We started walking, and soon we were in that room, and it was huge. At first, I didn't notice the chest on the gigantic pile of rocks.

When I climbed the hill I picked up the chest and brought it down to ground level and then we all gathered around and I opened it and inside was an old piece of paper that read: go through the door to your left and into the clearing, do the puzzle that opens the door and you will find the fourth piece to the shield of Zeus.

We looked around and didn't see any doors, but after a few minutes of looking, Danyelle spotted it and called us over. We went through the door and started going down the hall that was on the other side of it.

A few hours later of walking down one hallway after the afterward, we finally came out into an opening but we couldn't see any door that would lock and so we started exploring and soon found out that there was more here that had met the eye.

I started thinking about all the other times we had been in a clearing, so I checked for waterfalls, but there weren't any. Then I checked for vines and then I saw some at the far end of the clearing.

I went up to them and started pulling them off and saw that they were hiding the door alright but this time we had to find four pieces to the lever and a gem so I pulled the others over to me and told them what needed to be done.

As we investigated, it wasn't long before found the gem and now all that had to be found was the four parts of the lever and where to put the lever as well.

A few minutes later, Athero came running up holding what seemed to be the top of the lever, so I tried to put the gem onto the lever part and, sure enough, it screwed in.

Then suddenly they both came running up to me with lever parts in their hands and I put the lever together and I said "we just need one more".

A few hours of looking I gave up and then I looked in the distance and saw it...the last piece was on the other side of the clearing so I went to go pick it up and when i came back the others were waiting patiently for me and I put the last part together and started looking for the hole in the door where I had to put it.

Then I found it and stuck the lever in and pushed and then the others started helping me and then the door opened and we fell in.

We picked ourselves up and saw that we were in a small room with a few things in a corner and then I saw the chest among the things in the corner.

We walked up to it and then I opened it and inside was the fourth piece of the shield of Zeus and I put it into my bag and Athero pulled out his map and said it looks like the next place that we need to go to is mt. Rainier.

When we were ready I rolled a teleportation marble and we all visualized where we needed to go and a portal opened and we hopped through into totally different weather.

CHAPTER 6

MT. RAINIER

When we stepped out of the portal, the sun was in the sky mid-day and we knew we had to climb mt. rainier.

We looked around and after a good long walk; we were at the foot of the mountain and we started hiking up.

After hiking for about an hour, I slipped on a slope and fell into a cave and then I saw it...the glyph on the far wall shining brightly.

I told the others I found the passage; come on down. When I said that, I could hear the others come down the slope and land on the ground in front of me.

When they landed, we walked up to the glyph, and we all touched it at the same time and we were all sucked all at once.

Then we landed in a heap and as we got up, we noticed we were in a gold room and I looked around and soon saw letters in the gold that read: go down this hall to the left and into the room of the music clef, past the stream that leads to the silver pond and you'll find clue number one.

We turned around and saw that there were six halls, two on the left, three on the right and one in the middle, so naturally we took the one in the middle, which led us right back to where we started.

So we then went to the first one on the right and it did the same thing, so we took the remaining one on the right and it led us to a hallway.

As we were walking down the hallway, we noticed the walls began changing from brown to a golden color and then to a red and I knew we were going farther into the earth than the mountain.

After ten minutes of going through this, we came into a cave that was humming in different tunes and I knew we were in the cave of clefs and we went past the cave and soon we were in another hall.

We started down this hall but soon I started getting a lot darker than it was and pretty soon it was almost pitch black and we had to feel our way through by holding onto the walls.

We felt around and I said "there has to be torches around here somewhere" and then my hand found one and then we continued as I lit the torch and I noticed we were in a tunnel that was about to end and as we neared the end, I put out my torch and we came out into the open where we found that there was a silver spring so we knew what we had to do and that is to follow it.

After twenty minutes of following the river it split in two and I saw a waterfall on side and nothing on the other and we went with nothing so we continued walking and found out that the path that we took was the wrong one and so we backtracked and went down the other one and soon we came to the pond but the pond had a waterfall attached and I knew that we would have to go behind the waterfall and the clue was behind there.

We climbed the rocks behind the waterfall and saw that there was a room behind it and in that room was a chest.

I went up to the chest and opened it and read it: slide down the slope but not off the edge, don't lose hope and cross the ledge down the hall and through the door you'll find the second clues note at the end of the corridor.

At that moment, the floor tilted, and we started sliding and before we knew it, we were sliding down a slope that ended in a chasm, and then I saw a torch on the side and it was on a metal post that was set into the rock so as I was about to fall off the edge I grabbed the rod and pulled myself to the side and saw the others falling out of control.

I told them to grab onto something solid and to hold on and they started looking around and right before they were going to go off the edge; they grabbed a hold of a rock on the side of the wall.

Once we were all on the same side, I realized that we all had to be on the other side and one by one; we crossed.

Once we were all crossed over, we started crossing the ledge and soon we were in the middle of the ledge and I noticed that the middle was missing and so we held onto the rocks at the top of the wall and crossed that way.

Once we crossed, we saw we were in a small half room and at the end was a hallway and as the first clue said go down the hall and through the door and the second clue's note will be at the end of the corridor.

We started down the hall and pretty soon we had found the door and we went through the door and on the other side there was emptiness so we fell until we hit ground and I heard Danyelle say, "I'm starting to get tired of this."

We got up and saw that we were in a corridor and in front of us at the end was a chest so I went up to it and opened it and inside was an old paper that read: through the field and past the waterfall that is green and into the caves that hold aquamarine, and past the shut down machines and you'll find the clue number two.

When we got down reading a door opened behind it and we knew we had to go through it and when we did, we saw we were in a field but in this field there wasn't one waterfall but two so we started looking to see if one waterfall was green and then I saw something glinting from the ground and I picked it up and saw that it was glass...clear glass.

I looked at it and glanced through it and it made the ground a different color so I put it up to my eye and looked at the waterfalls and saw that one of them was green and one was blue.

I went past the waterfall that was green and found a cave that was full of gems that was also a greenish color called aquamarine.

We started looking at them and saw that they were incredible and I wanted to take one home, but I didn't know what that would do.

So I left it alone, and we started walking again and pretty soon we came to a yet another hallway that led to another field but this one was a lot different for one it had old machines in the corner and there was an old chest maker in the other corner and I knew I had to find the chest in this pile of junk and so we fanned out and started looking around.

When we couldn't find anything, we started looking for ways to get it to appear thinking that it was invisible and we just couldn't see it.

Then Danyelle motioned for us to come to her and she pointed to the appear, of the machine and I saw the chest and I pulled it out and put it on the ground.

Then I blew the dust away and opened the dang thing and saw the tablet inside still shining like it was new and we all covered our eyes until the shine was gone and then I picked it up and read it: down the hill and into a cave where it's red and blue do a puzzle with keys a few past the gold and silver chest and through the tunnel of fireflies and the note to the third clue you shall find.

When we finished reading, we noticed that there were hills all over the place, but only one led to a cave.

We climbed the only hill that led to a cave and then the descent was easier and also faster and before we knew it we were at the cave and we peered in and all we could see was black with a bit of red and blue light.

We started walking in the dark and soon we came across the red and blue crystals it had mentioned in the clue and we stopped to look at them and soon we were noticing we were getting hypnotized again and I quickly phased out of it and had to wake up the others by pulling them out of the room.

When we got to the next room, the others were still out of it so I knew I had to do this one alone and I noticed that there was a lever in the center of the room and I walked up to it and looked on the side of it to find that I had to find five keys.

I started looking for the first one and quickly found it in a box, but to be quite honest, that was the easiest one to find.

I put the first key into its lock and turned it and a light went on in front of me and then I started looking for the second one and it was not a box, as easy as the first one because it was in a room that disguised itself as a closet.

I went to put the second one into its lock and turned it and the second light went on and I started looking for the third but I saw Athero was stirring so I went to him and asked if he was okay and if he could help me find the rest of the keys and he nodded and together we searched for the third key and we both found a key at the same time.

He went to me and gave the key that he had found to me and I went to the lever and put them both in and turned them both and then two more lights lit up and we started searching for the last one.

When we finally found the last one we had a hard time getting it because the last one was hanging from the door, luckily the top of the door wasn't very high and all I had to do was reach up to get it and then I went back to the lever and put the key into it and turned it.

When the last light went on, I felt rumbling and then I turned around to see a new door opening.

We went through the door and found ourselves in another hallway, but this one was a lot shorter than the others that we have been through and at the end was a vast room that was filled with gold and silver chest.

We continued walking and soon we were in another hallway and this one led to a brick wall so I touched it and the whole hall lit up and after that happened I got sucked through and I was in a hall that was full of them and the room was lit up almost like it had torches in it.

That is when I noticed the chest in the corner room and I went to It, opened it and read it as soon as the others were with me.

When the others came through, I read: go through this door and past this room of gold and you'll find the third clue. As I was reading a door started opening and I noticed we had to go through it and soon we were in a hallway like the one that we were in and we started walking down that hall and after a few minutes of walking down that hallway we came into a room that was huge and I saw at the top of one pile of gold was the chest.

I started walking up to the gold but I couldn't because I would walk a little and then I started sinking, so I looked around and saw a ledge that I could climb.

I pulled myself onto the ledge and then jumped onto the top of the gold pile, grabbing onto the chest as I landed and as I sank; I pulled the chest down with me and I walked out with it in my hands.

When I got back to the open, I set it down, and I opened it and inside was the third tablet and it was as shiny as the others and like the others it dimmed down enough to read and when I looked at it, I read: down this hallway through the hole in the ground and into the water across the field and through the water and you'll find the note to the fourth clue.

We started down the only other hallway that there was and almost immediately I felt myself dropping and then I was in water.

As I was treading water I felt the water ripple and then breathing and I said "Danyelle, Athero is that you?" When they didn't answer, I started swimming as fast as I could only to find out that there was no shore.

I dove and saw light coming from the other side of the water and so I started swimming towards it and as I looked back; I saw what was in the water with me and I was terrified.

I started swimming faster and sooner than expected I came out on the other side and there to meet me were Danyelle and Athero.

We started off the shore and soon we were in a hall that was teeming with plant expansion and as I was walking past, there was a plant that was moving and looking at it as I went through.

As we were walking, I could see a light coming up ahead and soon we were in a doorway that in front of us was a field and this field was huge.

We started walking across the field and then we came across another underground forest and I thought we had to go in there until I saw the corner of the field that was hidden.

So I went to it and saw that it had a waterfall and then it clicked through the water...it meant waterfall.

I went up to the waterfall and saw that there was a rock path that led behind it, so I went up the path with the others trailing behind me.

When I was through, I saw I had found a secret room and I started going through things and soon I found what I was looking for...the note.

When I opened the chest that it was in, I picked it up and read it: back through the water and open the locked door and past the Valspar galore and you shall find the fourth clue.

We walked back how that we came to the waterfall and had a look around and soon we had found the first locked door and we saw by the pictures on the wall that there were four pieces that had to be found and we started looking.

Almost as soon as we started we found the first part of the lever which wasn't far from the gem and then I tried putting them together but they didn't match so we kept looking and soon found another part.

When we found the second part we tried putting those two parts together but no can do.

So we just kept on looking and then Danyelle found the third piece and I said" toss it to me" and I held out my hand and to my surprise a lightning bolt came out and grabbed hold of the piece and pulled it to me like a magnet.

I put the piece connected to the first and third piece and now all we needed was the fourth piece.

A few moments later, I found the last one and connected it to the others and then put it into the door and turned it like a key.

With that the door opened and we went through only to find more darkness with flashes of red and purple so we thought it could be amethyst and ruby or garnet and then I got a better look at it and saw that it was Valspar and I knew we were in the Valspar galore room and we just walked to the opposite door.

When we did, we walked out into a room that had nothing in it except a chest that was in the middle of the floor.

I walked up to it and opened it and inside was the tablet that was shiny as ever.

As soon as the shine went down, I started reading: down the hall to the right, past the stairs to the left, down the stairs ahead and then turn back and you'll find the note for the fifth clue.

We started towards the hallway that was on the right side and started going down that hall and after a long few hours

THE SHIELD OF ZEUS

we stopped for a rest and then I said, we better get to moving again.

We started moving again and pretty soon we had reached the end of the hallway and it started getting wider and more room was available.

We continued walking until we saw a door up ahead, and in a few moments, we were there. Then we opened it to find that it only led to another hall. We looked around and saw that everywhere else seemed to lead to a dead end.

So we went through that door and into the hallway beyond. As we were walking, I noticed that there was a staircase that seemed to be on the walls, but I didn't see how.

Suddenly, as I thought to myself, a staircase appeared to the left, and we turned onto them just as the clue had instructed us to.

Then we went forward after we had climbed the stairs and stepped foot on the top step and we started walking down that hallway.

After a few minutes of walking down that hallway, we were in a room that didn't seem to be out of the ordinary, that is until Danyelle sat in it.

When she sat in it, the seat leaned back and a door opened to yet another set of stairs, so we set off down those stairs and found ourselves at a drop off, so we jumped and landed not too far from where we were.

When we got up, we started having a look around and that is when I saw the box that I knew had to have the note.

I picked it up and read it to the crew: take the left-hand door here and then take the first right door and go across the field and on top of the hill you will find the fifth clue.

We turned to where the door was supposed to be but didn't see any door until Danyelle went over there to see it closer and she got sucked in.

We both got together now and went up to it, and we didn't even have to touch it. As soon as we got close, it began sucking us in.

When we got sucked in, we went to another hallway and right away we started seeing doors, but none of them were right sided.

So we kept on walking until a few hundred feet from where we started was the first right sided door so we went through it and found ourselves in a room that had a locked door that had three bars so I looked at the instructions and I tried to do what the instructions were telling me to do.

Then finally Danyelle came over and moved a couple of switches and it clicked and then a button flipped open and I pushed it, only to reveal three keyholes.

We started searching for the first key and within a few minutes Danyelle had found it and she brought it to me so I could put it into the lock and so I did and I turned it and then we got back to work on finding the second key this time and then Athero found it this time.

He brought it over, and I put it into the keyhole and turned it and then the first place I looked I found the third one and I put it into the lock and turned it and the door opened to a field.

I walked across the field and soon found the hill that I was looking for and I went to go up the hill and on top of the hill was a well and so I pulled the bucket up and inside the bucket was the fifth tablet but this one didn't shine because it was wet I presume.

I took it out of the bucket and read: through the field and out the locked door and through the hole in the wall and you will find the note to the sixth clue.

We started walking across the vast field and after about an hour we were still walking; a few minutes later, we reached a door, unsealed despite the note claimed, and went through it anyway. We started walking across the vast field and after about an hour we were still walking and went through it, anyway.

Emerging on the other side, we found ourselves in a distinct part of the field. We walked across and soon discovered another unlocked door; passing through, we found ourselves in another field.

We walked across this field and quickly found the door, but this one sealed, so we looked it over and I saw it needed four keys and a lever that was broken into three parts.

We started walking around looking for the keys and the lever pieces and soon Danyelle found the first out of three parts of the lever and she handed it to me and I put it into the lever hole and for once; it fit.

Then I went back to looking for the second part or a key and found a key so I went over to the lever and went to put the key into it and saw that I had to wait.

Then I heard my name and Athero came running up with a part in his hand and he handed it to me and I connected it to the first one and went to looking for the third part and soon I saw Danyelle running to me with the last part in her hand and she gave it to me.

I grabbed it from her and connected it to the others and then put the first key into the lever base and it went in and a light on the door went on.

Then I started looking for the next key and saw a shiny piece of metal on the ground so I went to it and it was the second key and I picked it up and went back to the lever and put it into it.

When I did another light went on onto the door and then I went to looking for the third key and soon found it near where we were and I went to pick it up but Danyelle beat me to it and she put it into the lever and the light turned on and we started searching for the last one.

After a few minutes, Athero came running with the last item. He gave it to me, and I let Danyelle insert it into the final keyhole. The lights illuminated, aligning themselves, and the lever moved forward independently, causing the door to creak open.

We went into the dark room and saw that we were in an old bunker of some sort, and then I saw the wrecking ball tied to a wall and I knew what I had to do. I went to the wrecking ball and cut the ropes and the ball rammed right into the wall, making an enormous hole, and then we moved it.

In its wake, we saw that there was a hallway and a note that I read to the sort, others; past the green and blue and past the red and purple and you will make do to find the sixth clue.

We looked around and saw that there was only one hallway forward, so we went into it and soon we were in pitch darkness.

Then I saw a faint light up ahead and we entered a cave lit by red, light-shining crystals—rubies, I realized—then we went into the next room filled with emeralds.

The emeralds shone brighter than that of the rubies, and there were more of them. As we continued walking, we found some amethyst that barely glowed, so we didn't even know that they were there.

As we were about to leave that part of the cave we saw one more crystal and that was some sapphires and they glowed immensely and they lit up that whole part of the cave and then we continued on our way and soon found our way into a huge room.

This room, filled with jewels and gold as it was and on top was the chest that we would normally have to look for so we started climbing the gold and about halfway the chest started sinking in the pile of gold and so did we so we hurried up and got to the top and grabbed the chest as it was going under and ran to safe ground.

I opened it and like most of the others the tablet shined and we had to cover our eyes until it dulled and then I picked it up and read it: through this door and down the hall through the hole and across the great fall and unlock the door and you'll find the seventh clue note.

We looked up to see a door opening into a hallway so we started walking through that doorway and we started going down that hallway and soon I couldn't see any of the others because it was pitch black...in fact I couldn't feel anything under my feet either.

Then I landed on solid ground and I started having a look around and then I saw it was dark. I picked up something I could use as a torch and I lit it and I saw it didn't help any and then I heard Danyelle and Athero behind me saying" what is this place?" and then I saw a sliver of light out of the corner of the place that we were in.

We went to the light and saw that it was a door. We opened it and went through it into the light on the other side. What we noticed was that we were in a field that had a cliff on it.

We went past the river running off the cliff and walked towards a door; the note stated that it's locked. We tried it, found it locked, and began searching it for answers.

Then I saw the pictures of a staff broken into three pieces and three keys next to it. I pointed out these pictures and then we started searching for the place where we would put the staff.

Then I stepped on a tiny hole and my leg twisted and I felt a slight pain in my leg and I looked down and saw the hole that the pole would go in.

I pointed out the hole to the others, and we started to looking for the pieces to the staff and almost immediately Danyelle found the first piece and I put it into the hole and it clamped down onto it and then I started looking for the second piece and then to my surprise after a good few minutes of searching I found the second one.

I went over to the first one and connected it to the second one and then, as I was about to look for the third one, when Athero came to me with it in hand and handed it to me.

I went to the other parts and connected the third and final part of the staff into the others and when I did; the keyholes appeared, and we started searching for the first key.

We continued searching the field and then I finally found the first one out of three keys. Then I brought it to the lever and put it in the side of it and one light began glowing.

Then we started looking for the second key and Danyelle started branching off and going her different way and then suddenly she bent over and picked up...the key.

THE SHIELD OF ZEUS

She came back to the group, and I said, "well done." I went back to the lever and put it in and the second light went on and we started looking for the third and final key.

We didn't have to search long because the key appeared in the keyhole after the other two were in and the third light went on and they all moved into a line and then the door opened revealing the note that I read to the others: in the next room is the clue but you'll have to look hard dude.

As I was reading, the door opened and revealed a small room that had many smaller rooms attached.

Each of us started searching each of the rooms and when we would get down with one room, we would go to another until we had searched all the rooms and not found anything.

Then I sat against the wall and I started sinking down to the ground and then I noticed a room that we hadn't checked yet and so I walked up to it and I felt a shiver go up my spine as if I had passed through something and then I knew that is exactly what I did because the others started calling out my name and I said "follow my voice".

Then they passed through because they came running up to me and they said "you found it". My confusion lasted until I looked left, saw the chest, and we gathered around it. I opened it, and the clue's shine was so intense it took a while to fade.

As soon as it did, I read the clue to the others: past the hall and down the stairs into the clearing and past the wares up the silver stairs and down the gold and you'll find the eighth clue's note.

We started walking past the only hall to the side and down the hall in front of us and soon came across some stairs going down that was made of stone and we went down and then we continued after that and came to a door and when we opened it we saw we were in yet another clearing.

We walked around the clearing until we found another door that we ended up going through and it had a lot of gold and copper coins in it.

So we knew that this was the wares that it mentioned in the clue and we saw a silver staircase going up and we started walking towards it.

We went up the stairs and soon found ourselves in another hallway with a set of gold stairs a little ways down a hallway to the left and so we went down that hall and down those stairs and found ourselves in front of a wall and so I stuck out my arm but before I could touch it; the wall opened into a room and we went through.

When we did, the hallway closed behind us and we looked around the room and saw that this room was the room that would have the note to the eighth clue in it.

So we started looking around and soon we found the chest that held the note in it.

I opened the chest and inside was a piece of paper that I read to the others: through the door on the right and past the door on the left, down the falls and past all the calls and you will find the eighth clue.

We started walking again and as we were going towards the wall doors started opening and we knew we couldn't go through them and they were all on the left and we kept going and then suddenly a door on the right was about to disappear when I pulled the others through it.

As Danyelle was going through as the last person, the door closed and I noticed we were in another room, but in the distance I could hear thunder...but that couldn't be right.

We were underground and then I knew what it was...a huge waterfall. We started walking again and soon we came to a river, so we walked down the river and saw just how big it was and we knew what had to be done again.

We started looking for something to go down the river in and soon we had something for each of us. I put my barrel in the water only to find out that it had a hole in it and so I went looking for another one and soon as I had I put it into the water and I got in because it floated and I started going down the river and then I put the lid on and screwed it shut and then I went over the edge.

Once I reached the bottom, I listened for the others to come down and then I saw them. As they were coming down, I watched them come down too.

When they landed, they came tumbling out of their barrels and then they walked up to me as if nothing had happened and then we started off again.

We started walking past a few empty caves when I started hearing my name being called out to me by a woman, but I couldn't see anyone and then I saw that this was the call and it stopped a few minutes later.

Then it started on Danyelle and she almost went for it until I told her what it thought and she turned away and then it stopped for her as well.

Then I began for Athero and then instantly stopped because he threw a rock at the caves and we moved into the next room where the gold chest was.

We walked into the next room and saw the chest in the corner and I went to it and I opened it while everyone gathered around and I read: go through the river and down the side of the lava down the stairs and you'll find the ninth clues note.

We started towards a door that was at the end and soon we were in another hallway and it was light inside of this one and soon we were in a room at the end of the tunnel like hallway.

When we got to the end of the hall, we saw that there was a river in the middle of the room and it was small, so we could cross it.

We walked up to it and started wading into it. As we did, the water started getting deeper and deeper, as if there was more water coming into the river.

So we hurried and crossed before it drowned us and as we were going up to land, a big tidal wave came across the river.

Then we took a deep breath and started walking again and soon came into another hall that was only a few meters long and then we emerged into a room that ended in lava and there was a channel going down to the left.

We followed the channel and stayed away from the lava because it was so hot that you would get burned by standing next to it.

We saw a doorway that was open to the left and it had stairs going down and curled around and we took them because it looked like the path we were taking was going to end so we went down the stairs and it led to a small room with the chest in it and I opened the chest and it held a note that read: go through this door and down the hall through the first door on the right and then the first one on the left and then past the fire flume and you will find the ninth and final clue.

We went through the door and started going down the hall and saw that there was one door in this hallway, but it was on the wrong side of the hall.

We just kept on walking and then I saw the door on the right side and I went through it only to find myself in another room and it held not one thing(aka it was empty).

So we started through the hallway at the back of the room and it had one door as well and this door was on the left and so we went through that door and found ourselves in another room that was filled to the brim.

There was one thing different about this room than the others I will point out, though it had a lever on the wall ahead of us. So we pulled that lever and the lever turned around with us on it.

We were now in a room that had a spiral flame going up into the air about a hundred feet and anyone that got close to it would get vaporized.

Then I noticed the keyholes by the door and I saw we needed three and they couldn't be behind the flame, so we started looking around where we were and soon I found the first key and I put it into the keyhole.

To my surprise, there was a small bit less flame and then I figured out that every key makes less flame, and the last key will make it go out.

We started looking for the second key for about an hour and soon after that was over; we had found the second key.

I put the second key into the second keyhole and turned them both, and the flame cut in half.

Then we started looking for the last key and soon found it hidden in a crumbling stone and I put it into the keyhole and turned and the fire went out, revealing a door on the other side.

We went forward and started through the door and as soon as we went through; the keys began popping out and soon the fire was back and we had nowhere to go but forward.

We could hear the fire roaring now and the tunnel we were in now was lit with torches and we started following that path.

At the end of the tunnel we saw a room that was about the size of a master bedroom and I went inside and inside the room was the chest with the last clue in it.

I waited until the others were next to me and then I opened the chest and we had to shade our eyes for a few seconds until the shine dimmed and then I picked it up and read: this is the final clue for this piece of Zeus's shield, go to the stairs at the end of the hall in front of you and then after a few meters turn left then immediately turn right and soon you will reach the note that will tell you where the piece is.

We started walking and after a few minutes of walking we came to a hallway and we could see the stairs in front of us and so we went down this hall and soon came to the stairs.

When we went up them, we almost immediately leveled out and then in a few meters, we took a left and then the passageway almost immediately turned right.

Then the floor gave out, and we went falling for what felt like a hundred feet and then we landed hard and I could barely move because I hurt all over and then I started rubbing my hands together and soon I had sparks and I didn't feel hurt anymore.

We started walking around and saw that we had fallen into a room with a couple of chests, but we knew that none of them were the right ones, so we went through the door at the end of the hall and started walking again.

Then we came out into a room and this one had one chest in the center of the room and it had a silver base and gold outline and I knew it had to be the one.

I waited for the others to catch up to me and then I opened it as the others were gathering around me and I picked up a piece of paper that was inside and read: the piece is not far now, all you have to do is go past the river and down the slope and into the caves that mope past the red and blue and get the next piece will you.

We started walking again and soon we started seeing ourselves getting closer to a river that wasn't as small as the last one, but it wasn't big either.

We started across the river, but the same thing started happening. The river began getting deeper as we went along and then as we were nearing the other side; we saw a title wave coming, and we hurried up and barely had enough time to get back on land again.

Then we moved forward and saw that we were on a hilltop and we started our descent slowly, and then we saw that this was the slope.

We were then at the bottom and I saw some caves about ten yards from us and so we started walking that way and soon we were at the caves and saw they were covered in water and then I started thinking "so that is why it's called the moping caves."

We walked in the caves and soon we were walking deeper into them and soon we were walking and saw a shimmer of green and I knew it had to be emerald but to my surprise; it was peridot and lots of it.

Then I saw some sapphire and there was rubies attached to some of them and I knew it was them it was talking about and soon I was walking past and we came out in another part of the cave that didn't seem to have anything in it except for a few chests and I knew that one of these chests had to be the one with the shield piece and I went to open it and saw the burn mark and I knew that two of these had bombs in them and the third had the piece in it.

We checked the other two boxes for burn marks and only one other one had them so we opened the one that didn't and saw the fifth shield piece and I put it in my bag and I heard a clink and that meant that they had fused together and then Athero pulled out his map.

now it said Yellowstone and then I rolled a portal marble and then Danyelle threw a drachma inside it and we visualized where we wanted to go and the portal opened and we went through into bright sunshine and we took a quick look around and saw that we were in a large field by a lake and we started looking around for a cave of some sorts and after a few minutes of splitting up, we all came back together.

I started looking for the cave while the others started making camp and I said we will camp here for the night and went over the hill to the left and as I did; I spotted a mine not too far from where we were and I went to it and went in.

When the others went to wake me up in the morning they were in for a surprise for I wasn't there and they started looking for me and that is when they saw the same mine and they went up to it and saw footprints in the mud and they were human and fresh as if they'd made it the night before.

Athero noticed the tracks were leading into the mine, so he went in himself and soon he saw Danyelle was following him.

He turned the corner and saw that there was a boulder in the way so Danyelle tried to move it and to Athero's astonishment it started moving and then it stood up and they saw it was a rock troll and we had no way to fight him so we did the only thing we could do and that is to run as fast as we could in another direction and try to lose him.

Athero then hid in the shadows as Danyelle went on by and Athero pulled Danyelle into the shadows right as the troll was going by and then we spied Zack and they went up to him and she asked, "where in Hades have you been?"

I answered, "I've been looking for the glyph and I think I might have found it," and I motioned for them to follow me as I began walking back into the darkness. They quickly went after me so they wouldn't lose me again and soon they had caught up with me and we started walking together. Soon we came into this big room and it had a large door in it and it had something shining behind it and I said, behind that door is the glyph but I can't find a way for the rock to collapse out from in front of it.

We started looking around and soon Danyelle came up to me and pointed at a lever hidden in a corner and then I remembered I could control electricity and I pushed on it with my hands and it began lighting up and then it rolled aside. When it did we saw it was a portal and so we knew it would teleport us to where we needed to go and we jumped in and saw a swirl of light and we got dumped onto the ground on the other side.

We stood up and noticed that we were in yet another field and I realized we were still in Yellowstone and we started searching for another cave and as we were searching Danyelle fell through a hole in the ground and I went over to her and saw that she was okay and then I yelled down to her and asked what she saw and she answered "I'm in a corridor and It might be our way in". I had to have a look for myself so I jumped down and started down the corridor with Danyelle on my heels and then I heard a splash and I knew that Athero had jumped down as well and then he was right beside me.

We walked down the corridor together and saw that it led into a fork and we talked it over and took the one on the left and soon found out that it led to the same place as the others, a single tunnel.

We went into the tunnel and soon saw that it was a puzzle to get a door open. I saw a lever in the middle of the room and I went up to it and saw that it had three lights on it and three holes in it.

I started to look around for some kind of straight metal item and found this long pin looking thing and so picked it up and tried to put it into the hole but it wouldn't fit so I put it down and started looking again.

Then I spotted a poker in the corner and I picked it up and tried it but it wasn't the right one either so I just kept on looking then I saw a glinting out of the corner of my eye and so I turned my head and saw the first piece on a barrel so I picked it up and put it into the first hole but it was a little big so I tried the second hole and it fit perfectly.

I started looking again and then I saw a pin that looked like it would fit into the first hole and then I saw the familiar glint out of the corner of my eye and I looked at it and saw the one for the third hole.

I picked it up and put it into the third hole but it was too big for it so I put it into the first one and it fit nicely in the first hole and so I went back to looking as soon as the light went on.

A few minutes of searching later, I spotted the third one, and I grabbed it and put it into the third hole and the third hole light lit up.

When the last light lit up, the door started moving, and we came face to face with another portal and we hopped aboard and soon we were flying into another tunnel and the first thing that I saw was a pillar that had a shield on it with a statue of Zeus on top of it and I knew we had to be getting close.

We continued to walk on the path we were on and soon we were in a room that had a portal, but this one was a little different because there were statues on both sides of the portal and I knew that this was the final portal.

I let the others catch up before going up to the portal and then we all jumped in at once and when we came out again we were in a cave that wasn't like the others and on the far wall was a replica of Zeus's shield.

We started looking around the room because we still couldn't see the emblem that would eventually take us to the next shield piece.

We started looking around the room and saw a lever that already had two of the three keys in it, so we started looking for the third key and I soon found it in a barrel near the exit.

I put the last key into the lever and soon the rock on the other side opened up revealing the glyph and we walked up to it and were about to touch it when it pulled me through without even touching the rock and I landed hard with the others right on top of me.

CHAPTER 7

AN END TO ENDS

When we got up, we saw we were in a tunnel and so we started walking and soon came into an immense room. As soon as we got into the room, we started having a look around and in a moment we started to see words writing themselves on the walls and they read: down the hall and up a flight of stairs through the crystal doors and then you will find the first note to the first clue.

We started through the doors on the left and soon we had found the hall that we were supposed to go down but the hall didn't seem to have an end so we just kept walking until we came to a door like hole and we went through it and then we came to a flight of stairs that we going down and I knew that this was the wrong one and so we kept going until we came to another set of stairs but this one was going up. We knew this one was the right one.

We started going up the stairs when we heard a thump, and we looked up and saw a boulder running down towards us, so we went running back down the stairs and swung around a corner.

We waited for the boulder to pass, then we finished going up the stairs and as soon as we were at the top, we saw the crystal doors that we were supposed to go through. We walked up to them and I noticed the lock on them, and there was a lightning bolt symbol on them.

Then it crossed my mind that I had to use electricity to open the gates. I put my hand up to the symbol and slammed the symbol down, making sparks.

When I did this, the gates opened, revealing a large crystal room that had a throne in the center along a wall. We started looking around, and soon noticed that there was a chest in the corner. I walked up to it, and went to open it but it sent me flying. I walked back up to it and looked closer. When I did, I noticed that there was an aura around it. Then I motioned for Danyelle, because she had a talisman with her.

She went up to it and went through her talismans, and when she found the one she was looking for, she put it up against the chest and it dispelled the aura. Then I went up to the chest and went to open it again. This time I could open it.

When I opened it, I looked inside and saw a note. The note read: Through a hole behind the throne you will find a staircase that has never shone up the stairs, and on the right behind door number three there you will find the clue you'll need.

We looked around and saw the throne, and I went to look behind it. I saw that there was a hole there. I motioned for the others to help move the throne. As we did, the hole revealed itself. We went through the hole after the throne got moved. When we got through, we moved to see that we were in a room with brilliant light.

I went to look where the light was coming from and seen light was coming from the walls. "It must be light outside," I said. We started up the stairs and noticed that the stairs weren't shining. Instead, the stairs were a dull gray, as if made from granite.

As we were going up the stairs, we noticed everything started looking tiny, as if from far away, and we saw the stairs were actually a lot longer than they looked. When they ended, we found ourselves in a hall that seemed to never end and in the first hundred feet, there was nothing but doors on the left. Then we knew we weren't supposed to enter any of those doors.

Finally, we found the first door on the right, but we had to go on the third door. After another hundred feet, we finally found the second door on the right. It had a door next to it, that was the third door on the right. We went through the door that was the third on the right. Inside was a minor puzzle that required one key.

We started looking for the key immediately, and soon Danyell found it. She handed it to me and I put it in the keyhole, and turned it. When I turned it, the gears started turning, and it brought up a chest.

I opened the chest, and inside was a silver tablet. It read: Through the door to the left, past the music that's made in bass clef. Past a river of molten ice, there you'll find something really nice. We turned to look but couldn't find any door in sight. So we started feeling the wall, thinking it was a trick wall, and sure enough, Danyelle's hand went through the wall, then we followed suit and went through the wall ourselves.

When we did, we found ourselves in a hallway that seemed to last forever and then we started hearing a low humming that seemed to illuminate from the walls themselves.

As we got to the other end of the hall, which had taken a long time, the humming stopped and we came into a clearing and in the middle of the clearing ran a red-ish blue river.

We looked for a way across but could find none and so we started glancing around and I noticed a rusty-looking lever so I went up to it and then I noticed the keyhole in the handle on the left, right, and top?

I knew I had to find the three keys that went with the lever and so we started looking for the first key and then I saw a piece of paper on the ground said, only when you quit, all will reveal.

I sat down and as soon as the others saw me sitting; they asked what I was doing and when they heard my reply; they sat down too. Then the most amazing thing happened. There was a shimmering in the air and the three keys appeared out of nowhere. We grabbed them and put the keys into the keyholes and I turned them and when I did; we noticed that there was a pathway in the water that we could walk through.

We ran through the pathway right as it was closing and then we started walking again. We started walking down the pathway that was on the other side of the river. Soon we were in another room and in that room filled with pottery, there was a chest in the corner.

We went up to the chest, and I opened it and picked up the golden tablet that read: go under the archway of the golden rock and through the rooms filled with silver and gold lines, unlock the thing that has the lock and past the cart that belongs in the mines and you'll find the next clue.

We started walking again and soon we could see the gold shimmering in the distance but it didn't seem high enough to be an archway and when we came up to it we saw it wasn't the archway instead we arrived in a room that was full of gold and at the end of the room was a gold door.

At first we thought the door was closed, but it turned out to be a crack so we went through it and soon we saw some more gold glinting in the distance and this one was higher and I knew it was the arch of gold.

We walked closer and saw it was the arch and man did it sparkle. We started walking again and soon we were walking down another hallway until we were in a room full of crystals.

We continued walking and soon we found the room that was shining so brightly that it almost hurt my eyes and when our eyes adjusted to the light; I saw that there were lines of gold and silver everywhere.

We went forward into the unknown and we started searching for a thing that needed to be unlocked. After an hour of walking, we came to a door that had an emblem of a lightning bolt on it and I knew that this was the thing that had to be unlocked.

So I put my hand on the emblem and I could feel the energy surging into my hand. I pulsed with my hand and the door flung open and we went through, or at least we tried.

Once the lightning bolt was gone an arrow appeared and I knew it had something to do with Athero so I had him come up to the front and he put his hand on the tip of the arrow and it shimmered and the door opened and started walking again.

As we were walking, Danyelle discovered a railway and so we started following it until it came to a dead end at a wall so we looked at the wall and I noticed it had a hole in it in the center.

I started peeling at the hole and made it bigger, so I continued until it was big enough to climb through. When I climbed through, I found that there was a mining cart on the other side and it was on its side and I knew it was the mining cart from the note.

Then I walked around to the other side and I saw it had the tablet that was the next clue that read: go to the right and down the hall and past the crystal pears and past the voices that call and you'll find the last piece of the shield of Zeus.

We turned to the right and saw a door appearing and we headed to it as it started disappearing. By the time we got to it, the door was almost gone, but we barely slipped through.

When we got through to the other view, we saw we were in a long hallway, so we started walking and after about an hour we started getting tired; then the hall curved and I could see the end.

When we came out of the end of the hallway, we saw we were in a room with crystals, but these crystals didn't look like pears...more like plums.

We kept on walking and soon found another room that also had crystals in it but again they didn't look like pears.

They looked like apples and so we just kept on walking and then I saw the vines on the wall and I had a flashback about the last time I saw vines on the wall.

I pulled on the vines and sure enough, there was a puzzle there, so I started looking around for the lever and then I looked down and saw a little stubble that I was stepping on.

I started looking around for a pipe that could be a part of the lever so I could pull it and soon found it in the room corner on a box.

I picked it up and put it into the hole and pulled it, but it didn't budge, so I started checking it out and noticed that it was the first of two pieces of the lever.

I started looking again and saw the second piece on the other side of the room and so I went to go get it and soon found out that it was an illusion.

When I went to grab it, my hand went right through it and disappeared. Then I noticed that the second piece was on the other side of the room where the first one was and when I went to grab it, this time nothing happened.

I picked it up and put it with the first piece and it melted together right in front of my eyes and then I saw it needed two keys, one on each side.

I started looking for the first key and after a few hours of wandering around the room, Athero found the first out of two keys and he gave it to me and as I put it in a light lit up green.

We started looking again and soon found the last key and I put it into the last keyhole and then the second light went on and a door opened revealing a lit room that was filled with a yellow light and we knew that this had to be the room with the crystal pears.

We looked around and then I said, guys time to go before we get hypnotized by the crystals. They both turned around, and we started toward the door and saw that it started closing.

We barely slid under the door and made it to the other side when the door had shut. We started walking across the room and after a few minutes;I started hearing someone started calling my name.

I started going towards it and then my friends stepped in front of me and then re-read the note and I started understanding.

We walked out of that room and went through the door in front of us and soon we were walking down a hallway and then the hallway just ended in a wall of dirt.

Then I looked up and saw the last piece of the shield and I took the cap off my marker and used my sword to pull it off the wall and then I put it onto the rest of the shield and then It started glowing and then creases disappeared and it became whole again.

We picked up our last marble and rolled it as we thought of camp and a portal opened and as we went through, Danyelle dropped a drachma and we teleported to camp Demi-god.

CHAPTER 8

A GOODNIGHT'S REST

We went to go find Chiron and soon found him eating lunch and as he saw the shield of Zeus; he stood up and started pulling us away from the rest of the camp. Then he asked, "so you got it did you? Now listen, Olympus is in the second dimension, but hurry."

We nodded and then Chiron said "wait you'll need these and as he handed the red marbles to us he said these are like the ones, you were using but they are called dimension marbles they will bring you to the dimension that you have to go to and you will be there momentarily and one more thing to activate them roll them into something."

He handed over ten marbles each, and we were about to roll the first one when Chiron said "this is the third dimension".

We rolled the first marble and thought into our heads of the second dimension, and then we felt a yank that pulled us into a black portal.

what we found on the other side of the portal was a giant mountain that had an elevator that was the size of a human.

We stepped into it, and it automatically started going up. When it stopped, we noticed we were at the top of the mountain, but higher still was Mt. Olympus. We started climbing up the stairs and after about an hour; we reached the first gate, but there were still more steps.

So we pushed the gate open and started climbing again. We climbed for about another hour and then we reached another gate, but still no Olympus, so we opened the gate and kept climbing.

We walked for about another hour then we landed ourselves at yet another gate and up ahead we could see two more gates than Olympus was ahead so we pushed open that gate and kept on walking and after about thirty minutes we landed at another gate and we saw we were getting closer to Olympus and so we pushed open that gate and then ap ahead of us was Olympus and as we went through the doors that led to the courtyard we started walking towards the palace.

When we walked the gods of Olympus looked down at us and when Zeus saw his shield he motioned for me to come closer and as I did, he said to me "you did well to return my shield" and then the shield grew and we knew our jobs done for now and we were about to go back to the camp when Hermes came bursting in and whispered in Zeus's ear.

Zeus turned to his brother Poseidon and told him that the trident of Poseidon has gotten stolen and then he knelt down on one knee and said to us" you did such a good job at finding the pieces of the shield of Zeus that I Poseidon am putting you in the position of finding my trident."

We nodded and rolled the marble into the wall and we said bye,and returned to the black portal to the other side. When we came out on the other side, we saw Chiron was waiting for us and when he saw us he smiled and said "well done".

Then we said our goodnights and headed off to bed because I had a feeling that in the morning we had to do the same thing with the trident of Poseidon the next day and as my head hit my pillow, I was out like a light and when I woke up the next morning; I went to see Chiron.

CONCLUSION INFO

---

concludes in the trident of Poseidon,

SNEAK PEEK

Chapter....1 the mission

We went up to see Chiron only to find a crowd of campers around Chiron and they were staring at us with disgust and we started pushing through to find what was wrong.

When he saw us he motioned for us to go inside and then he said to us" someone seemed to have leaked the fact that you are going on another quest."

Donald Carter lives in the bustling small city of Cape Girardeau, where he enjoys walking by the Mississippi river and reading. He also loves going to the library and the book rack in his free time.

www.ingramcontent.com/pod-product-compliance
Lightning Source LLC
LaVergne TN
LVHW021829060526
838201LV00058B/3565